INDIA AT THE POLLS

WEINER, Myron. India at the polls: the parliamentary elections of 1977.
American Enterprise Institute for Public Policy Research, 1978. 150p
ill map (AEI studies, 202) index 78-15030. 3.75 pa ISBN
0-8447-3304-0. C.I.P.
Weiner gives a firsthand account of the 1977 Indian parliamentary election
that toppled Indira Gandhi and her Congress party from power for the first
time. He conceives the Janata party, with all its variability and vulnerability to fragmentation, to be a possible rival party in a developing two-party
system. He feels the repudiation of the 20 months of emergency and
authoritarian rule bodes well for the world's largest democracy. With the
Communist parties on their own, the election was less ideological and more
a single-issue election over democracy. The south supported Congress as
against the north, but there was no discernable urban-rural split. Indira
Gandhi's charisma seems to guarantee her opposition will remain a focus of
strong alternatives. Recommended for library acquisition at all levels.

INDIA AT THE POLLS

The Parliamentary Elections of 1977

Myron Weiner

221890

American Enterprise Institute for Public Policy Research
Washington, D.C.

Myron Weiner is Ford Professor of Political Science and a senior staff
member of the Center for International Studies at the Massachusetts
Institute of Technology. All photographs in this book were taken by
the author.

Library of Congress Cataloging in Publication Data

Weiner, Myron.
     India at the polls.

     (AEI studies ; 202)
     Includes bibliogaphical references and index.
     1. Elections—India.   2. India—Politics and
government—1947–   I. Title.   II. Series:
American Enterprise Institute for Public Policy
Research.   AEI studies ; 202
JQ292.W44   329'.023'5405   78-15030
ISBN 0–8447–3304–0

AEI studies 202

Printed in the United States of America

To Ajit and Lakshmi

CONTENTS

ACKNOWLEDGMENTS

I am grateful to the Center for International Studies at the Massachusetts Institute of Technology for funding my trip to India, especially on such short notice; to the officials of the Indian government who granted me a visa though they were aware of my hostility to the emergency; to numerous friends in Bombay, Hyderabad, Madras, Calcutta, and Delhi who made local arrangements for me; to my research assistants, Nikhil Desai and Robert Berrier, who helped prepare materials for the statistical analyses; to Professor Paul Brass for his editorial suggestions; and to the American Enterprise Institute for inviting me to write this small but I hope useful account of an event that was important not only for India but for the contemporary world.

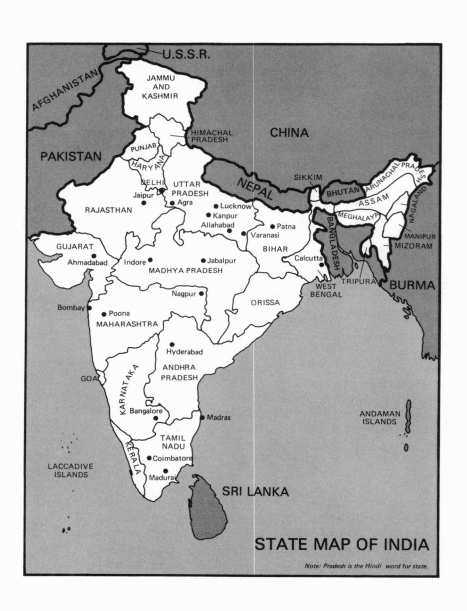

STATE MAP OF INDIA

Note: Pradesh is the Hindi word for state.

1
Introduction

The Indian parliamentary elections of March 1977 brought to an end thirty years of Congress party rule, eleven years of government under the prime ministership of Indira Gandhi, and twenty-one months of an emergency that had set the nation on an authoritarian course. If, instead of elections, a violent upheaval had marked this turning point, we might be writing about India's "democratic revolution." As it is, we are concerned with an extraordinary, even historic, set of events: An authoritarian government that appeared to be well entrenched called a genuinely free election, permitted political parties to openly seek electoral support, ended press restrictions, released the bulk of political prisoners from jail, and politically neutralized the police and civil administration. Not only that, but when it lost the election, the government quietly stepped down. This is all the more remarkable in that it happened at a time when most observers were sadly concluding that democracy had been premature in the Third World.

But then political developments in India have rarely been in step with those in other developing countries. From August 1947, when India became independent, to June 26, 1975, when Prime Minister Gandhi declared the national emergency, India was one of a handful of developing countries where the political process was open and competitive. Freedom of the press, freedom of assembly, competitive parties, honest elections, and a genuine respect for human rights prevailed, and neither the military nor the police played an independent political role—a rarity in the Third World. A single party, the Indian National Congress, or Congress party, dominated the political life of the country. Founded in 1885, the Congress party was the oldest political party in Asia and one of the oldest and largest non-Communist political parties in the world. India's great national leaders—Gopal Krishna Gokhale, Bal Gangadhar Tilak, Surendranath

TABLE 1

CONGRESS PARTY RESULTS IN SIX PARLIAMENTARY ELECTIONS, 1952–1977

Election	Vote (in percentages)	Seats Number	Seats Percentage
1952	45.0	357	73
1957	47.8	359	73
1962	44.7	358	73
1967	40.7	279	54
1971	43.6	352	68
1977	34.5	153	28

SOURCE: Press Information Bureau, *General Election 1977, Reference Hand Book*, New Delhi, 1977.

Banerjea, Motilal Nehru, Mohandas Gandhi, Chitaranjan Das, Subhas Chandra Bose, Jawaharlal Nehru, Rajendra Prasad, Sardar Vallabhbhai Patel—were all leading figures in the Indian National Congress. Under Mahatma Gandhi's leadership, Congress had become a mass-based movement with popular rural as well as urban support. The Congress organization reached into most of the provinces and districts of British India so that by 1947 it was virtually a parallel authority to the British raj.

With Jawaharlal Nehru (Indira Gandhi's father) as the independent country's first prime minister, Congress leaders took charge of the central and state governments in 1947. The Constituent Assembly, which wrote India's Constitution, was largely made up of Congressmen (as members of the Congress party are called). In the country's first national elections based on universal adult suffrage in 1952, the Congress party swept to victory both in the national Parliament (Lok Sabha) and in the state assemblies. And in each of the parliamentary elections that followed every five years, the Congress party emerged with a clear majority of seats (see Table 1).[1]

Opposition parties did flourish and from time to time some of these won control over state governments, municipalities, and other local bodies. Moreover, the Congress party itself embraced a variety

---

[1] For an account of the role of the Congress party since independence, how it won electoral support, and how the party functioned at the local level, see Myron Weiner, *Party Building in a New Nation: The Indian National Congress* (Chicago: University of Chicago Press, 1967). For an account of the development of the party at the national level, focusing on the organizational structure, see Stanley A. Kochanek, *The Congress Party of India* (Princeton: Princeton University Press, 1968).

of interests, ideological groups, and factions which, in their conflicts with one another, often turned to groups outside the Congress for support or broke away to form new opposition parties. To many Indians, certainly to members of the Congress party, India had developed a near unique political system—a "Congress system," which provided the country with stable authority, a regime committed to economic development, socialist planning, and secularism, all within a free-wheeling democratic process.

India was also one of the few developing countries that had decentralized power. The Constitution of 1950 had provided a federal system, under which considerable authority was allocated to the states. Moreover, while there had been conflicts among various ethnic-linguistic groups, India had avoided massive civil strife. Except in the months immediately preceding and following independence, and despite an extraordinary degree of social diversity, political life had unfolded peacefully.

Yet by the 1970s many of the distinctive features of the Indian political system appeared to be coming to an end. The government had become more and more centralized. Centrally controlled paramilitary and police forces were playing an increasingly important role, as was an intelligence apparatus under the direct control of the prime minister. State governments were controlled by the prime minister, at whose pleasure the state chief ministers held office.[2] At the same time, public strife was on the rise. Industrial strikes had proliferated; the universities were in political turmoil; a nationwide railway strike threatened to paralyze the economy. In one state there was a mutiny within the police; in the states of Gujarat and Bihar the opposition parties instigated popular agitations attacking governmental corruption, rising prices, and food scarcity and demanding the resignation of the state governments. The political system seemed unable to cope with severe inflation, an industrial recession, growing unemployment, and a slowdown of the economic growth rate. The system had, to quote Rajni Kothari, India's leading political scientist, produced "insecurity at the top (hence the continuous process of concentration of power into fewer and fewer hands) and unrest at the bottom (hence the rising torrent of protest)."[3]

With the declaration of the emergency in mid 1975, India ceased

---

[2] Since the states, like the central government, have a parliamentary form of government, the chief ministers are chosen by the majority parties in the state assemblies. After the state assembly elections of 1972 the prime minister, through her control over the Congress party, dictated the choice of chief ministers in the Congress-controlled states. On the eve of the emergency, Congress controlled fifteen of India's twenty-one state governments.

[3] Rajni Kothari, "Design for an Alternative," *Seminar*, August 1977, p. 12.

to be exceptional, or so it seemed. By reverting to a course familiar in developing countries, India had demonstrated, according to many observers both within and outside India, that a "soft" state was incompatible with the requirements of a late-developing economy. Perhaps, some sadly concluded, human rights in the sense of freedom of speech, freedom of the press, the right of assembly, and freedom from arbitrary arrest must inevitably give way in the face of rapid population growth, large-scale malnutrition, poverty and unemployment, gross inequalities of income, and rising popular expectations.

Background to the Emergency

Prime Minister Gandhi justified the emergency by asserting that the opposition parties had been resorting to extraparliamentary and extraconstitutional measures to force the Congress party out of office and had been inciting the police and armed forces to commit acts of indiscipline. But the prime minister's critics, including most foreign observers, believed that the emergency had been declared less to meet a national threat than to meet a challenge to her own power. What was the immediate background to the declaration of June 26, 1975?

Opposition agitation against the Congress party governments in both Bihar and Gujarat in 1974 and early 1975 had won considerable popular support.[4] Under attack and torn by factional divisions, the Congress government in Gujarat resigned, the state assembly was dissolved, and "president's rule"—direct rule by the central government, provided for by the Constitution—was proclaimed. Following a fast by Morarji Desai, a leading opposition figure, the central government agreed to hold elections in the state in June 1975. To fight this election, the opposition parties banded together to form the Janata (People's) Front (a name we shall encounter again) which, despite Indira Gandhi's helicopter tour throughout her state, won an important victory: eighty-six Janata seats in the state assembly against seventy-five for Congress.

Also in June 1975 the Allahabad High Court found Indira Gandhi guilty of violating the Representation of the People Act in her 1971 election to Parliament, largely on a series of relatively minor technical violations of the law. A few days later the Supreme Court gave her a conditional stay until her appeal could be heard by the full court,

---

[4] See Dawn E. Jones and Rodney W. Jones, "Urban Upheaval in India: The 1974 Nav Nirman Riots in Gujarat," *Asian Summary*, vol. 16, no. 11 (November 1976), pp. 1012–1033. The authors suggest that the Gujarat movement, known as Nav Nirman (social reconstruction), inspired the anti-Congress movement against the Bihar state government later in the same year. It attracted support from secondary school and college teachers, students, and the salaried middle classes. The agitation in Bihar was led by Jayaprakash Narayan.

but she was informed that she could not vote in Parliament while the case was under review, an anamolous position for a prime minister. Though the senior Congress leaders urged her to remain in office, there were widespread reports that quite a few members of her party believed Mrs. Gandhi ought to step down.[5] The opposition parties, encouraged by their victory in the state elections in Gujarat, announced that they would launch a national campaign for the prime minister's resignation, and several of the country's leading national newspapers also urged her to resign.

On June 26, Mrs. Gandhi struck against her critics within the Congress party, the opposition parties, and the press with her proclamation of the national emergency. Thousands of members of the opposition parties, including some of the country's most prominent political figures, and many members of her own party were arrested, the right of *habeas corpus* was suspended and the press censored, twenty-six political organizations of the left and right were banned, public meetings and strikes were declared illegal, and numerous foreign journalists were expelled. Parliament was subsequently called into session to ratify the declaration and to amend the electoral law retroactively so that the offenses committed by Mrs. Gandhi in her electoral campaign would no longer be illegal.

Within a few months the government took steps to bring about more enduring changes in the Indian political system. In late 1975 Parliament passed the Prevention of Publication of Objectionable Matters Act, which imposed restrictions on the press that would be independent of ordinances declared during the emergency. The government consolidated the wire services and created Samachar, a new government news service that would exercise control over both the collection and the dissemination of domestic and foreign news.[6] A

---

[5] Details of the opposition to Mrs. Gandhi within the Congress party were made public in testimony presented before the Shah Commission in December 1977. The Shah Commission (named after former Chief Justice of the Supreme Court J. C. Shah, who serves as its chairman) was appointed by the Janata government in April 1977 to inquire into excesses committed during the emergency. According to the Shah Commission, opposition to Mrs. Gandhi came from three prominent Congress members of Parliament: Chandra Shekhar, Krishan Kant, and Mohan Dharia. All three were arrested when the emergency was declared. See *Overseas Hindustan Times*, December 22, 1977.

[6] See Dileep Padgaonkar, "The Sad Story of the Media—How to Restore Their Credibility," *Times of India*, April 2, 1977. Padgaonkar writes that during the emergency the Ministry of Information and Broadcasting pursued three objectives: "Project the personality of Mrs. Gandhi and Sanjay Gandhi in the best possible light, highlight the gains of the emergency, and black out every news item that in some way hinted at popular discontent over the government's repressive measures." Padgaonkar notes that the ministry set precise "targets" for the number of leaflets and posters to be printed and the number of minutes of broadcasting time to be devoted to specific subjects and personalities.

number of ordinances were issued empowering officials to arrest individuals without disclosing the grounds for detention or arrest even to the judiciary. The Maintenance of Internal Security Act (MISA) was amended to provide the government with the power to detain political prisoners without charges even if the emergency were ended. The paramilitary Central Reserve Police and Border Security forces grew in importance,[7] as did the Research and Analysis Wing (RAW), an intelligence-gathering unit located in the prime minister's secretariat. The elections scheduled for March 1976, when Parliament would complete its five-year term, were postponed for a year. And in December 1976 the Constitution was amended to permit the government to prohibit "antinational" activities and to strengthen the powers of the prime minister in relation to the legislature and the judiciary.[8]

An underground opposition to the government developed during the emergency, but it hardly constituted a threat. There appeared to be a thriving underground press, but many of its members were arrested. In mid 1976 George Fernandes,[9] the most prominent leader of the underground and head of the railway federation, was picked up by the police and charged with conspiring to overthrow the government by violent means. Strikes were effectively prevented and, while in mid 1976 there was some vocal protest in New Delhi and other parts of north India over the slum clearance and sterilization programs launched by the government, there were no signs of any mass opposition.

In the latter part of 1976, the regime seemed to soften its stand. Fewer arrests were made, a number of opposition leaders were released from jail, press censorship was eased, and foreign journalists were readmitted with few restrictions. On the other hand the justifications being offered for the emergency gave it a more permanent ring. Initially, the emergency had been justified as a temporary measure to deal with a "threat to internal security" in accordance with a constitutional provision that permitted the government to suspend

---

[7] According to an analysis in the *Economic and Political Weekly* (April 9, 1977), central and state budgeted expenditures for police in 1976–1977 were 6.9 billion rupees as against 3.3 billion in 1970–1971, a rise of 109 percent as compared with an 80 percent rise in development expenditures during this period.

[8] *The Constitution (Forty-Second Amendment) Act, 1976*, Government of India, Ministry of Law, Justice and Company Affairs. For critiques of the bill written and circulated during the emergency, see *Nationwide Demand for Postponement of Constitution Amendment Bill*, New Delhi, 1976, signed by a number of academics, journalists, and jurists opposed to the emergency; and S. P. Sathe, V. M. Tarkunde, V. A. Naik, E. M. S. Namboodiripad, and V. K. Narasimhan, *Democracy and Constitution (Forty-Second Amendment) Bill* (New Delhi: Citizens for Democracy, 1976).

[9] Many Indian Christians have Western names. Fernandes's family comes from Goa, a former Portuguese colony.

fundamental rights under such circumstances. But now the prime minister and her supporters justified the emergency as a means of ensuring the country's economic growth, alleviating poverty, ensuring social justice, and so on—in short, as an instrument for dealing with many of the country's fundamental long-term problems. The Constitution (Forty-Second Amendment) Bill was approved by a Congress-party–dominated Parliament for the purpose of "removing the difficulties which have arisen in achieving the objective of socioeconomic revolution which would end poverty, ignorance and disease and inequality of opportunity." At the end of 1976 the prime minister declared still another one-year postponement of parliamentary elections. By early 1977 there seemed little prospect that India would have free elections any time soon or that the democratic process would be restored by peaceful and constitutional means.[10]

The Decision to Hold Parliamentary Elections

"Some eighteen months ago," began the prime minister in her radio broadcast to the nation on January 18, 1977, "our beloved country was on the brink of disaster. Violence was openly preached. Workers were exhorted not to work, students not to study, and Government servants to break their oath. National paralysis was propagated in the name of revolution."[11] So spoke the prime minister in what appeared to be a familiar restatement of her justification for the declaration of a national emergency. She then explained that the restrictions had been gradually eased, that "leaders and many of the rank-and-

---

[10] For accounts of the events leading up to the emergency and the institutional changes which subsequently took place, see W. H. Morris-Jones, "Whose Emergency—India's or Indira's?" *World Today*, vol. 31, no. 11 (November 1975); Richard L. Park, "Political Crisis in India, 1975," *Asian Survey*, vol. 15, no. 11 (November 1975); Norman D. Palmer, "The Crisis of Democracy in India," *Orbis*, vol. 19, no. 2 (Summer 1975); Norman D. Palmer, "India in 1976: The Politics of Depoliticization," *Asian Survey*, vol. 18, no. 2 (February 1977); Myron Weiner, "India's New Political Institutions," *Asian Survey*, vol. 16, no. 9 (September 1976); Rajni Kothari, "Restorng the Political Process," *Seminar* (July 1976); W. H. Morris-Jones, "Creeping but Uneasy Authoritarianism: India, 1975–76," *Government and Opposition*, vol. 12, no. 1 (Winter 1977). For an account of the way in which power was centralized within the Congress party prior to the declaration of the emergency, see Stanley A. Kochanek, "Mrs. Gandhi's Pyramid: The New Congress" in Henry Hart, ed., *Indira Gandhi's India: A Political System Reappraised* (Boulder: Westview Press, 1976). For an interesting attempt to place the emergency in the context of corporatist theory, see Lloyd I. Rudolph and Suzanne Hoeber Rudolph, "To the Brink and Back: Representation and the State in India," *Asian Survey*, vol. 18, no. 4 (April 1978).

[11]"Reaffirming the Power of the People," *Prime Minister Smt Indira Gandhi's Broadcast to the Nation*, January 18, 1977 (New Delhi: Ministry of Information and Broadcasting). For the complete text, see Appendix A.

file, who had been detained, have been released . . . press censorship has been relaxed and newspapers have been reporting the activities of people and parties. . . ."

Then in a stunning departure she declared,

> We . . . strongly believe that Parliament and Government must report back to [the] people and seek sanction from them to carry out programmes and policies for the nation's strength and welfare. Because of this unshakable faith in the power of the people, I have advised the President to dissolve the present Lok Sabha [Parliament] and order fresh elections. This he has accepted. We expect polling to take place in March.

Mrs. Gandhi went on to announce that "the rules of the Emergency" would be "further relaxed to permit all legitimate activity necessary for Recognized Parties to put forth their points of view before the people." She ended her address by saying: "Every election is an act of faith. It is an opportunity to cleanse public life of confusion. So let us go to the polls with the resolve to reaffirm the power of the people and to uphold the fair name of India as a land committed to the path of reconciliation, peace and progress."

After the prime minister's announcement thousands were released from jail, including her most prominent opponents (some of whom were members of the governing Congress party). She suspended press censorship and announced that public meetings would be permitted. But the prime minister also made it clear that the emergency was not ended, nor had civil liberties been permanently restored. As she said in her broadcast, for the duration of the election campaign the "rules" of the emergency would be "relaxed."

Why were elections called and why at this time, only a month after the government had announced another postponement? As far as we know the decision was made by Indira Gandhi herself, perhaps in consultation with a few close advisers—perhaps, some Indians believe, in the advice of an astrologer.[12] There is no evidence that the

---

[12] One state official in Andhra Pradesh interviewed by the author during the campaign thought this likely. "Astrologers have a strong hold on all of us," he said,

> even those like myself who are educated and like to think that we are scientific and without superstition. . . . There is an astrologer here in Hyderabad who regularly flies to Delhi to consult with Mrs. Gandhi. At least that's what he tells me and I have no reason to believe that he's not telling the truth. There are also quite a few prominent people here who consult him. There are some people around Mrs. Gandhi who call him to Delhi and pay his travel and expenses. Mrs. Gandhi says that she never calls for astrologers but sometimes they come in to see her

matter was discussed in the cabinet or that any of the senior cabinet members were consulted.

It was widely believed that Mrs. Gandhi was holding the elections for two reasons. First of all, by demonstrating the country's support, the elections would legitimize the emergency and the recent moves to institutionalize many of its features, including the constitutional amendment.[13] By "[cleansing] public life of confusion" they would establish the regime's domestic legitimacy, and that in itself would "uphold the fair name of India" before the court of world opinion. Even as the prime minister denounced the Western media and Western intellectuals for failing to understand that the emergency

> . . . I understand the astrologer told her there would be three generations of Nehrus in power. But he didn't say whether she should start counting from Motilal, her grandfather, or Jawaharlal. It depends upon whether you're counting presidents of the Congress party or prime ministers of India!

Indira Gandhi had high hopes for her son Sanjay.

[13] The amendment was passed in December 1976, a few weeks before the prime minister announced the elections. Some critics of the government have argued that the prime minister wanted the bill passed before elections were held since the government could not be sure that in the new Parliament Congress would again hold two-thirds of the seats, the number required for a constitutional amendment. In November the Indian press reported that the Forty-Second Amendment to the Indian constitution had been endorsed by *Pravda* in a statement that said that its aim was to "bring the basic law of the State into line with the changes in the country's economic and socio-political life." The *Pravda* article went on to say that

> in recent years, some outmoded provisions of the Constitution have been used by Indian reactionaries to fight progressive measures by the Indira Gandhi government. Thus in 1969 the Supreme Court attempted to prevent laws on the nationalization of big private banks from going into force on the pretext that they were unconstitutional. And in 1970 it tried to strike down new laws abolishing pensions to former princes and maharajahs. The Allahabad court was used in 1975 to declare Indira Gandhi's election to Parliament illegal. In this manner the reactionaries strove to turn the judicial system into a weapon for sabotaging progressive reforms.
>
> After a state of emergency was declared in June 1975, the country was faced with the immense task of strengthening democratic institutions and increasing their role in the country's sociopolitical life. With the passage of the amendment, Parliament's role as the body of supreme authority in the republic is confirmed. From now on its decisions cannot be challenged by the Supreme Court or by the higher courts of the states.
>
> The reactionary parties boycotted discussion of the amendment in Parliament. The progressive democratic forces, including the Indian Communist Party, expressed support for the bill's main provisions, declaring them to be in the national interests. . . . Progressive circles are in favor of turning the Constitution into an effective means of strengthening the country's democratic institutions."

Oleg Kitsenko, "Bill Passed," *Pravda*, November 6, 1976, p. 5, translated in *Current Digest of the Soviet Press* (American Association for the Advancement of Slavic Studies), vol. 28, no. 45 (1976), p. 23.

was necessary under Indian conditions to provide the country with stability and discipline, even as she explained that the "Westminster model" was no longer appropriate for India, her frequent interviews with Western reporters showed how sensitive she was to what they wrote and said.

Second, elections would provide Indira Gandhi's younger son, Sanjay, with an opportunity to establish his power within the Congress party in Parliament and thereby improve his prospects for succession to the prime ministership. Sanjay had already created a power base within the youth organization of the party, the Youth Congress. His supporters described the Youth Congress as a growing mass movement with the capacity to revitalize the aging Congress party, while his critics feared that the organization, which attracted many tough, opportunistic young people and which had developed strong ties with the local police, might become India's equivalent of a fascist youth corps. Moreover, though Sanjay held no public office, during the emergency he became a powerful influence within the government and was already regarded by many as second only to the prime minister.

Another factor that may have affected Mrs. Gandhi's decision to hold elections was the growing opposition to many of her measures within the Congress party. In Uttar Pradesh, Punjab, Haryana, and Bihar, Congress state legislators had met to protest the Forty-Second Amendment. The law minister had received 250 proposals for amendments from M.P.s, most of them Congressmen. The Congress parliamentary party had refused to accept constitutional amendments proposed by the government that would have transferred control over agriculture from the state governments to the center and removed the right of property from the Constitution. There had been political clashes between H. N. Bahaguna, the chief minister of Uttar Pradesh, and Mrs. Gandhi that had led to his dismissal, and Sanjay Gandhi had succeeded in obtaining the dismissal of Nandini Satpathy as chief minister of Orissa. In November 150 Congress M.P.s had abstained from voting on the decision to postpone elections a second time.[14] By calling elections Mrs. Gandhi may have hoped to obtain greater control of her own Congress party.

Why Mrs. Gandhi chose to hold the elections at this particular

---

[14] The sources for these indications of opposition to the prime minister within the Congress party have been assembled by Angela S. Burger of the University of Wisconsin in an unpublished paper, "A Himalayan Miscalculation: Analysis of Elite Control in the 1977 Indian Parliamentary Elections." Her sources are articles by Denzil Peiris in the *Far Eastern Economic Review*, the *Economist*, and *Blitz*. I am grateful to Professor Burger for making this paper available to me.

time is a matter for speculation. Only a few weeks earlier Prime Minister Bhutto of Pakistan had announced that his country would hold elections, thereby making Pakistan the only democratic country in the region. This may have precipitated Mrs. Gandhi's decision. Then too, President Carter's human rights campaign may have had real impact on a government that professed adherence to human rights and free elections. Finally, there were indications that the economic situation might worsen in the next year or two and that if elections were to be held at all, this was as propitious a moment economically as any likely to arise in the near future.

It seemed unlikely that the splintered opposition parties could organize themselves into an effective political force with a common platform and set of candidates on such short notice. They would also have difficulty raising money, given the likelihood that they would lose. Would the business community—many of whom were profiting from the emergency and some of whom feared retribution—provide the opposition with funds? In a country with 320 million voters and 542 parliamentary constituencies, the campaign was bound to be expensive.[15] Moreover, though censorship had been suspended, surely the press would be cautious. During the emergency, the government had successfully pressured the managing boards of several newspapers to remove editors known to be critical of the government—and it continued to maintain control over its own consolidated news agency, Samachar.

Beyond the handicaps of the opposition, Mrs. Gandhi had a variety of reasons to expect the elections to give her an overwhelming victory. The harvest had been comparatively good. Prices, though rising, were increasing at a substantially lower rate than in the period prior to the emergency. Some of the measures taken under the government's Twenty-Point Program to improve the lot of the urban and rural poor had been successful.[16] Housing sites had been allocated to Harijans (ex-untouchables), land had been redistributed to the landless, bonded labor had been abolished, rural indebtedness had been reduced, and alternative housing had been provided for some urban squatters. While each of these benefits of the emergency had its detractors, the government, at least, viewed many of its key measures as both successful and popular. Sanjay Gandhi, meanwhile, seemed to have a real following. He had been acclaimed by the chief

[15] For an account of what it costs to run parliamentary elections in India see Eric P. W. da Costa, "The Cost of an Election," *Surya India*, March 1977, pp. 13–21.

[16] For the texts of the government's Twenty-Point Program and Sanjay Gandhi's Five-Point Program, see Appendixes B and C.

ministers of the states he had visited and large crowds appeared at his public meetings. The press coverage of his own Five-Point Program for social reform, which included family planning, was enthusiastic, and his Youth Congress was attracting, at least according to reports in the press, tens and even hundreds of thousands of followers. Sanjay's promise, and Mrs. Gandhi's hope, that the Youth Congress, built upon a popular base of energetic young people, would take over the Congress party seemed within reach.

All of this, we know now, was fantasy. Like many authoritarian regimes, this one was unaware of how unpopular many of its policies and programs were and of how little popular support the regime had. The lack of effective feedback in itself might not have threatened the government had it not made the extraordinary decision to test its popularity by holding elections.

Observers have speculated as to why Mrs. Gandhi so grossly overestimated her government's popularity and failed to take steps, as have authoritarian leaders elsewhere, to ensure her victory. Some have concluded that Indira Gandhi, her authoritarian behavior during the emergency notwithstanding, remained a true democrat and honestly viewed the emergency as a temporary measure. Others believe she was misled—perhaps intentionally—by leaders of the Congress party and officials of the intelligence agencies about her prospects for victory in an open contest. Perhaps at a deeper level Mrs. Gandhi was faced with a genuine dilemma: after thirty years of democracy India's politicization was so great, there were so many political organizations articulating so many interests, that to maintain a lid on newspapers (and printing presses) and public meetings during an election campaign would have required a very high level of authoritarian control— even greater, probably, than that already imposed. For Mrs. Gandhi, therefore, the choice was between permitting free elections and ending all semblance of democratic legitimacy. Whether or not a fundamental personal commitment to democracy was the decisive factor, Indira Ganhdi may also have been uncertain about how much support she could continue to expect from the military and from her own associates within the Congress party. The extent of dissidence at the highest echelons of her party was to become apparent earlier than Mrs. Gandhi ever expected.

The Nation Reacts

Within a few days of Mrs. Gandhi's announcement, two events took place which were to have a decisive effect on the outcome. The first was the announcement by four of the opposition parties that they had united to form the Janata party, which would contest nearly all of the seats. The four parties were:

(1) *The Congress O.* The largest of the opposition parties, the Congress O. (for Organization, or the "Old" Congress) had split off from Mrs. Gandhi's Congress party in 1969 after a two-year period of intense conflict between Mrs. Gandhi and a group of state Congress party leaders popularly known as the Syndicate. Though the schism was initially factional and personal, it was given an ideological coloring when Mrs. Gandhi declared her opposition to the private banks, the former princes, and the "right-wing" Congress party bosses and her support for populist measures to eliminate poverty. At first the Congress O. retained the support of a majority of the state Congress party organizations, but it rapidly lost support after it won only 10.4 percent of the vote in the parliamentary elections of 1971 and Mrs. Gandhi's Congress won two-thirds of the seats in Parliament. In the 1972 state assembly elections, the Congress O. declined to 6.7 percent of the vote while Mrs. Gandhi's Congress party won 70 percent of the state assembly seats. But the Congress O. continued to have many prominent national leaders, including Morarji Desai and Sanjiva Reddy.

(2) *Jana Sangh.* Formed in 1951, Jana Sangh was committed to Bharatiya, or Indian culture, but it was widely viewed as a pro-Hindu, anti-Muslim, and anti-Pakistani organization. Its greatest strength was in the Hindi-speaking states of northern India, where it participated in five coalition state governments after 1967 and had the support of shopkeepers, white-collar workers, and some of the professional classes. It was particularly strong in the capital city, where in 1967 it won both parliamentary and municipal elections. In 1971 it polled 7.4 percent of the vote and in the next few years appeared to be gaining popularity.

(3) *The Bharatiya Lok Dal* (BLD). In 1974 Charan Singh brought together seven small parties to form the BLD. The most important of these were the Bharatiya Kranti Dal, whose main support came from the more prosperous agricultural classes in Uttar Pradesh, and the Swatantra party, supported by business and by the landlords and princes of Rajasthan and Orissa. Largest of the seven constituent parties, Swatantra polled 3.1 percent of the vote in 1971.

(4) *The Socialist party.* Formed in 1971, this was a descendent of the Congress Socialist party, founded in 1934 as a socialist

group within the Indian National Congress.[17] Ideologically it incorporated Marxist, Gandhian, and democratic socialist elements. It won 4.5 percent of the vote in the 1972 state assembly elections. While the Socialist party had organizations in all of the northern states, its greatest strength was in Bihar, Uttar Pradesh, and Maharashtra. Among its leaders were George Fernandes, Raj Narain, and—though he was no longer actively engaged in politics—the elderly and much revered Gandhian socialist Jayaprakash Narayan.

These parties had worked together before, but now for the first time they agreed to submerge their individual identities. The new party would be led by Indira Gandhi's old rival Morarji Desai, whose removal from the cabinet had been one of the events leading to the Congress split in 1969. It would include on its governing committee the country's leading opposition figures, most of whom had only recently been released from jail.

Given the long history of aborted efforts to unify the opposition, the creation of the Janata party came as a considerable surprise, but circumstances conspired to make it possible. The opposition politicians knew that an electoral defeat would probably ensure the institutionalization of the authoritarian measures, and the short time given by Mrs. Gandhi for the election campaign forced them to act quickly. Jayaprakash Narayan, who had initiated the preemergency campaign against the prime minister in Bihar, spurred events when he announced that he would not take part in the campaign unless the opposition united.[18] Since the Congress party had won earlier elections with less than a majority of popular votes—and since the four parties that now formed Janata had already won a not inconsiderable 27.6 percent of the vote in the 1971 parliamentary elections[19]—many thought that a unified opposition could make very substantial inroads into the Congress party's parliamentary strength.

The biggest surprise, however, came on February 2, when a senior minister in Mrs. Gandhi's cabinet, Jagjivan Ram, resigned from the

---

[17] The Socialist party was formed through the merger of the Samyukta Socialist party (SSP) and the Praja Socialist party (PSP). The PSP, which had emerged after independence under the leadership of Jayaprakash Narayan, had become the leading non-Communist opposition party in India by 1957. But the party was torn between those who wanted to remain equidistant from the Communists and the Congress and those who wanted to work more closely with the Congress party. The more militant group split off to form the SSP, which emerged as the stronger of the two Socialist parties in the 1967 elections and again in 1971—after which the two reunited.

[18] *Times of India*, January 20, 1977.

[19] For a detailed breakdown see Table 3, p. 68.

government, denounced the emergency, and announced that he was forming his own political party, the Congress for Democracy (CFD), which would support Janata party candidates.[20] Ram, a long-time Congress leader and minister, was a prominent figure in the politics of the state of Bihar and a leader of India's Harijan community. Ram was particularly harsh in denouncing Mrs. Gandhi for destroying democracy within the Congress party. He noted that during the emergency party officers had been appointed, not elected, and that in many states with Congress party governments the chief ministers had been chosen by the prime minister, then approved by the state legislative assemblies, rather than elected by the assemblies. Two state Congress leaders, both former chief ministers of their states, joined Ram. Hemvati Namdan Bahuguna, a fifty-four-year-old Congress leader in Uttar Pradesh, India's most populous state, a trade unionist and a popular figure among his state's Muslims, and Nandini Satpathy, a forty-six-year-old social worker and political leader from the eastern state of Orissa, also announced that they were resigning from Congress to join the newly formed Congress for Democracy.

Ram's resignation evidently led Mrs. Gandhi to fear widespread defections from the Congress party. In an effort to minimize defections she and her close supporters concluded that most of the sitting members of Parliament should be allowed to run again. The result was that the Congress Election Committee, which selects candidates—or, to use the Indian expression, allocates tickets—had to deprive Sanjay Gandhi's Youth Congress of the large share of tickets it expected.[21] While it was initially anticipated that the Youth Congress might be given 150 to 200 tickets out of 542, the party leadership decided to give them only about 20, including one safe constituency in Uttar Pradesh for Sanjay himself. Jagjivan Ram's resignation thus deprived

---

[20] Jagjivan Ram's resignation statement of February 2 was also signed by H. N. Bahuguna, Nandini Satpathy, K. R. Ganesh, D. N. Tiwari, and Raj Mangal Pande. The statement is primarily an appeal to fellow Congressmen. For the complete text see Appendix F.

[21] Congress candidates for parliamentary seats are nominated by the District Congress committees to the Pradesh (state) Congress committees (PEC) which then forward their recommendations to the Central Election Committee (CEC), a subcommittee of the Working Committee (the executive committee) of the party. The CEC is made up of the members of the Congress Parliamentary Board, five members elected by the All India Congress Committee, and the prime minister as an ex-officio member. In some elections the CEC accepts the recommendations of the PEC, while in other elections it intervenes directly in the selection process, especially when the state Congress is factionally split. In the 1971 parliamentary elections it was generally understood that the PECs and the state chief ministers played a secondary role in candidate selection compared with the CEC and Mrs. Gandhi herself, who was particularly concerned with nominating candidates loyal to her.

Mrs. Gandhi of the opportunity to redistribute power within the Congress parliamentary party in favor of her son. It also tended to strengthen the position of some of the state Congress leaders, who were now given considerable influence in the allocation of tickets to their own Congress supporters. Moreover, the elimination of the Youth Congress as a significant force in the elections also neutralized the state police—with which many of the Youth Congress leaders were closely allied—as a political force. Finally, Ram's resignation provided an important psychological boost to the Janata party, for it not only opened up the possibility of substantial Janata inroads into the Harijan and Muslim vote but also created the possibility of further defections from the Congress party.

Thus, within two weeks of Indira Gandhi's announcement, it was clear that these were likely to be free elections and a real race. Among the early indications that Mrs. Gandhi might be in trouble were the public rallies organized by the Janata party in India's major cities. The largest of these was held on February 6 at Ram Lila grounds in New Delhi, where several hundred thousand people turned out to hear Jagjivan Ram, Jayaprakash Narayan, and a cast of Janata party leaders. Mrs. Gandhi's rallies were not so well attended and she was often booed by members of the audience.

Still, it was generally assumed in early March that Mrs. Gandhi's Congress party would win, though perhaps by a substantially reduced majority. The economic signs—for those who believed that the state of the economy would be the decisive determinant of how the electorate voted—seemed reasonably propitious for the government. The country had built an impressive buffer stock of food, industrial production had substantially increased in 1976, the performance of the government-run public sector plants had shown significant improvement, a successful program of oil exploration had led to the commercial production of crude oil from wells off the coast of Bombay, foreign trade had increased enough to give the country a favorable trade balance in 1976, there had been a very substantial increase in the country's foreign exchange reserves, and wholesale prices had increased by only 8.5 percent during the year. *Commerce*, a leading business review published in Bombay, estimated that real national income had increased by 6.5 percent in 1975 and by an additional 3 percent in 1976.[22]

Moreover, it seemed likely that, even if Congress lost some of the urban areas where there was resentment over the loss of civil liberties, including the right to strike, Mrs. Gandhi would win the

---

[22] "India: A Year of Consolidation," *Commerce* (March 5, 1977), p. 282.

support of the countryside. Given the improved economic situation, it seemed unlikely that the countryside would turn against the government on political grounds; censorship, political arrests, the banning of strikes, the weakening of the judiciary, it was said, could hardly affect the masses of rural people. Most members of the Indian government held the view that in a developing society a largely illiterate peasantry is more likely to be moved by economic considerations than by abstract arguments about democracy and civil liberties. Sanjay Gandhi had made this point only a few months earlier when he had called for postponing the elections on the grounds that the country wanted "bread not elections."[23]

But Janata and Congress for Democracy leaders concluded that the political question, not economic issues, should be foremost in the election campaign. "The choice before the electorate is clear," said the Janata party manifesto. "It is a choice between freedom and slavery; between democracy and dictatorship; between abdicating the power of the people or asserting it; between the Gandhian path and the way that has led many nations down the precipice of dictatorship, instability, military adventure and national ruin."[24] Lofty phrases, but would they mean as much in rural India or in the city slums as they might among the educated classes in the cities?

[23] "Hamen Roti Chahiye, Chunao Nahin" (We want food, not elections), read banners in Hindi at a rally in support of the prime minister's Twenty-Point Program held in Badwani constituency in the state of Haryana in November.

[24] Election Manifesto 1977 (New Delhi: Janata party, n.d.), p. 1. For extended extracts from the Janata manifesto, see Appendix H.

PART ONE
The Campaign

2

The Campaign Gets Under Way

This account of the 1977 campaign is based on the author's observations, interviews, and researches during his tour of India in the weeks before the election. In five widely scattered cities—Bombay on the west coast and Calcutta in the east, Hyderabad and Madras in the south, and New Delhi in the heart of northern India—he talked to civil servants, candidates, campaign workers, newspaper editors, and people in the street, attended campaign rallies and visited ward offices, collected campaign literature, listened to the radio, and followed the local press. He watched the election returns come in in the capital, New Delhi. The result is not a systematic assessment of the campaign in every region, but a firsthand report of what happened in representative regions of the country.

Meetings and Media

In a country with a high level of illiteracy and a correspondingly low newspaper circulation, a radio system that is controlled by the government and reaches only a fraction of the population, and a government-controlled television system that broadcasts only to selected urban areas and a handful of villages, participation in an election campaign largely takes the form of attendance at public meetings. In this campaign the turnout at public meetings was clearly greater than in any of the five preceding parliamentary elections. Described by newspapers as "mammoth," it often ran to hundreds of thousands.

Public meetings for political purposes had been banned before the relaxation of the emergency, and after the ban was lifted they proliferated like mushrooms after rain. At the Ram Lila Grounds in Delhi, at the Maidan in Calcutta, on public grounds in cities, towns, and villages across the country, crowds gathered to hear the candidates speak. Marina Beach—which stretches the length of the city of Madras along the Indian Ocean, and where people regularly come to relax after the heat of the day—was the scene of some of the largest rallies. It was estimated that half a million people came to hear Indira Gandhi here, and probably as many turned out for the Janata leaders. In northern India the Janata meetings, often lasting till two or three in the morning, were unusually large and enthusiastic. They gave credence to the early newspaper reports that a Janata wave was sweeping the country.

When Indira Gandhi announced that the emergency would be relaxed (leaving open the ominous possibility that the repressive measures might be restored after the elections) the press, cautiously at first and then more boldly, described the Janata party campaign and the popular support it was receiving. Most of the working journalists were opposed to the government. While few actively canvassed for him, many provided financial support for George Verghese, a popular journalist who was standing for Parliament in a constituency in Kerala. One-time press secretary to Mrs. Gandhi, Verghese had been dismissed from his position as editor of the *Hindustan Times* as a result of pressure from the government.

The government's policy of cutting off all government advertising in newspapers that were opposed to the Congress party further embittered the press. Asked to explain the policy at a press conference in Cochin, Kerala, Indira Gandhi replied: "Why should we give advertisements and support to newspapers owned by big industrialists who have enormous money at their disposal?" The *Indian Express* answered her in an editorial headed "Ads as patronage," on March 9. It claimed that Mrs. Gandhi's attitude was

> contrary to government spokesmen's repeated declarations in the past regarding the basis on which government advertisements are given to newspapers. . . . If the main consideration in selecting the media for government or public sector advertisements is not their value or utility as media, but the political or other attitudes of the owers . . . this will mean a blatant abuse of public funds for partisan ends.

Such a policy would pose "special dangers to a free press in an increasingly state-controlled and state-owned economy like ours," the editorial concluded.

The *Indian Express* and the *Statesman*, two of India's largest circulating English dailies, were prime targets of the government advertisement policy. Both papers had resisted government domination during the emergency and both supported Janata. After Mrs. Gandhi ended press censorship, both newspapers boldly printed accounts of governmental excesses during the emergency, and both reported the growing wave of sentiment against Congress candidates. The circulation of both papers rose. It was claimed that the circulation of the Delhi edition of the *Indian Express* (which is published in several cities simultaneously) increased some threefold during the election campaign.

Two of the major English dailies, the *Hindu,* published from Madras, and the *Hindustan Times,* published from New Delhi, continued to support the government. The *Times of India,* which publishes editions from both Bombay and Delhi and is one of the largest Indian newspapers, was cautious at first but by mid campaign began to pay increasing attention to the popular support for Janata candidates.

Posters and Graffiti. In Bombay—and it was typical—banners and streamers were tied across streets, especially the main thoroughfares of slum neighborhoods, and every wall, large and small, was covered with election posters and graffiti. The Congress theme was simply, "For progress and stability—vote Congress." Congress posters either showed Mrs. Gandhi alone or paired up pictures of her with pictures of the local Congress candidates. The posters of the prime minister printed by the Congress party during the emergency had all but disappeared, including the ubiquitous one of a stern-faced Indira Gandhi above the inscription, "She stood between order and chaos. She saved the Republic." The campaign posters, by contrast, portrayed a benign, mother-like figure in a flowing sari. But the horatory posters printed by the government during the emergency for display at bus stands remained, solemnly urging: "Talk less, work more," "There is no substitute for hard work," and "The Twenty-Point Program is a blueprint for progress."

Janata had fewer posters than Congress (they are an expensive campaign item) but more graffiti. "Our pledge—bread and liberty— vote Janata" was a favorite Janata slogan. Among the others scrawled on the walls of Bombay and Hyderabad were: "Save democracy— vote for Janata party," "Problems are plenty, points are twenty, results are empty," "We are curtailed—freedom of speech, freedom of press, fundamental rights, freedom of association—to restore them forever vote for Janata party," "Our political leaders are still in jail— release them at once—vote for Janata," "A ballot for Janata is a bullet for democracy," "For civil liberties, freedom of the press, independence of judiciary, vote for Janata party," and "What do you want? Freedom or slavery? For freedom elect Janata party." In Amethi, the constituency that Sanjay Gandhi was contesting, Janata graffiti

An emergency poster still displayed in Calcutta during the election campaign.

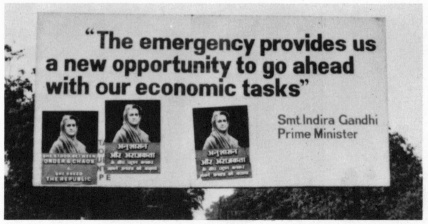

Poster displayed in central New Delhi during the emergency.

Banner supporting Mrs. Gandhi displayed in central New Delhi during the emergency.

An Election Commission poster widely displayed all over India. Photographed in Madras.

A Janata poster, New Delhi.

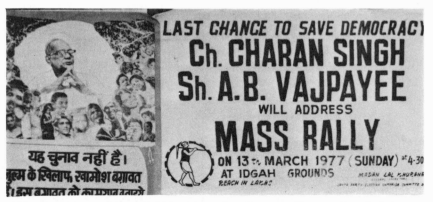

A Janata poster, New Delhi. After the election Charan Singh became home minister and A. B. Vajpayee became minister of external affairs.

Graffiti, Hyderabad, Andhra Pradesh.

Graffiti, Hyderabad, Andhra Pradesh.

claimed that the election was a fight between *Samajwad* and *Sanayavad*, democracy and dynasty.

Most common of all were stencilled drawings of a farmer and plow, the symbol of the Janata party; the corresponding Congress graffiti said "Support Indira Gandhi—Vote cow and calf" (the symbols of the Congress party), also with a stencilled drawing. And throughout Bombay one encountered an official poster produced by the national Election Commission, which to some had an antigovernment ring: "Vote without fear—your vote is secret."

Janata Mobilizes

India's high levels of political organization and political participation (the two obviously go together) are invariably revealed in an election campaign. The Congress party could rely on organizational machinery that reached into almost every corner of the country. Virtually every town of any significant size had a local party office and party workers. Traditionally the local Congress organizations had support from large sections of the local rural gentry and from the local business community. The party had at its command a network of contacts in the country's villages. It had jeeps, and it had money. In contrast, the Janata opposition, so recently a disorganized string of warring parties, drew on less established sources of support and was faced with formidable problems of organization, communication, and finances.

The Janata party was born in jail. It was in Indira Gandhi's prisons that members of the diverse groups that had failed time and again to form a united front against Congress in the past came to know one another and realize the possibility and necessity of working together. This theme, reiterated by Janata workers in various places, was best expressed by Chakradhar, secretary of the Janata party in Andhra, south India's largest state. The author first met Chakradhar in 1961 when he was a member of the Rajya Sabha, the upper house of the Indian Parliament, and a leader of the small but active Socialist party in the state. Chakradhar spent fourteen months in the Secunderabad jail near Hyderabad.

> There were about 500 party workers in my jail. About 100 belonged to the RSS [the Rashtriya Swayamsevak Sangh, a pro-Hindu militant youth organization closely associated with Jana Sangh], the Jammaat-e-Islami [an orthodox militant Islamic group], or were Naxalites [the radical wing of the Communist movement in India]. The remainder were Socialists, members of the Jana Sangh, or former Congressmen. The jail conditions were not too bad and the jailers

28

had no objection if we had meetings. So in the jail we had classes on ideology, economics, and politics and how the various groups might come together. The most important change was the way the various parties came to accept the Jana Sangh workers. We emerged from jail not as a coalition of parties but as a single party.

Some Janata workers spoke almost with nostalgia of the comradery they had known in jail; the mood they described recalled the solidarity that had united the Indian nationalists in British jails during the independence movement.

Its leaders freed and united, the Janata party set about drawing up a slate of candidates. Ad hoc committees were hastily formed in each state, made up of the constituent elements of the party, and state election committees were formed to process the recommendations made by the district units of the newly formed party. In some areas these units consisted of members of several parties and in others exclusively of members of one of the constituent parties. The process was somewhat chaotic, especially since the Janata party did not have a formal constitution and the constituent parties did not formally dissolve themselves to merge with Janata until after the elections. Moreover, many of the party organizers, including most of the candidates, had just been released from jail. Candidate selections had to be made hastily since there were only a few weeks between the time Janata was formed and the time nomination papers had to be filed with the returning officers of the Election Commission.

The Janata party drew its cadres not only from the constituent elements of the party, but also from college and university student organizations, especially in the towns of northern India. Many students who had not hitherto taken part in political affairs volunteered as canvassers in both urban and rural constituencies in support of Janata candidates. Thousands of young people fanned out on bicycles into the countryside to work for Janata candidates. The trade unions, resentful of the government's restrictions on strikes and opposed to its policy on annual bonuses, were even more active than usual in industrial constituencies. Members of the bar associations, whose network extends into small towns in rural India as well as the larger cities, supported Janata candidates, and in some of the larger cities lawyers demonstrated publicly, manifesting a degree of political involvement they had not shown since the independence movement. State government employees and teachers too were more involved in the campaign than they had been in earlier elections, particularly, as we shall see, because of their forced involvement in the government's family planning program.

In short, even before the election returns revealed that there had been a substantial increase in turnout over the 1971 parliamentary elections, it was evident that the emergency and the strongarm tactics of Mrs. Gandhi and her son had politicized sections of the electorate. The way this worked to Janata's advantage can be illustrated by a closer look at what happened in one constituency in Bombay—a Congress stronghold.

Janata in Bombay North Central. The Bombay city Congress organization was widely regarded as one of the most effective party machines in the country and played a particularly important role in fund raising for the national party. In the 1960s the Bombay party organization had been dominated by S. K. Patil, a Congress leader with close ties to the business community, but when Congress split in 1969 Patil had been forced out of the party by Indira Gandhi. Since then the city Congress machine had been run by Rajni Patel, who like his predecessor emerged as a major figure in the national party organization by virtue of his domination of the Bombay city organization. As part of her strategy of preventing independent centers of power from growing up within the party, Mrs. Gandhi abolished the Bombay Congress Committee and incorporated the city organization into the state party. Rajni Patel's position was, therefore, substantially eroded.

Only a few months before the election Sanjay Gandhi took another step to reduce Patel's position by berating him publicly for independently raising money for the party. This was a clear signal to the business community that funds should be contributed directly to the central Congress party organization in New Delhi. Some businessmen privately complained that they were being pressured by the government to make large contributions to the Congress party by purchasing, at 10–20,000 rupees per page, advertisements in so-called souvenir volumes published by the party.

At a time when gasoline was selling for two dollars a gallon in India, Congress party candidates appeared to be well supplied with jeeps and automobiles. They had more posters, banners, pamphlets, and leaflets than the opposition and could fund larger numbers of party offices throughout the city. Nevertheless, it was widely reported that the abolition of the independent Bombay Congress city organization and the removal of Rajni Patel had thrown the local Congress organization into disarray.

Though the pro-Soviet Communist party of India was officially supporting the Congress party, the Communist trade unions in Bombay were critical of the emergency and of the Congress government policy of suspending bonuses. The Muslim League was officially supporting the Congress party, but it was widely understood that many of the Muslims in Bombay were concerned over the government's compulsory vasectomy program. By and large, the city's middle class was known to be hostile to the emergency and to the Congress party. All in all, even Congress supporters thought they would be lucky if they could win three or four out of the six Bombay seats, though all of the incumbents were Congressmen.

The most important prestige constituency in Bombay city is Bombay North Central. There Ram Jethmalani, a former president of the India Bar Association, was the Janata candidate, running against Haribhau Ramchandra Gokhale, the law minister who had engineered the legal and constitutional innovations during the emergency. Shortly after the emergency was declared a warrant had been issued for Jethmalani's arrest and he had fled. Granted asylum in the United States, he had continued to be an outspoken critic of Indira Gandhi's government. After the Janata party nominated Jethmalani for the Bombay seat, he flew to his constituency. Though the warrant was still pending, Gokhale advised the government not to arrest Jethmalani and to allow him to remain free to contest the elections.

For one day, or more precisely from six one evening till three the next morning, the author accompanied Jethmalani on his speaking tour through this sprawling constituency. His son Tony, who had returned from his studies at Oxford to work for his father, was with him, as well as his wife who sat next to him on the platform at each of the public meetings. There were not fewer than several thousand people at any of the six meetings the candidate attended that night. At one, which continued till two in the morning, there were upwards of 50,000 people. The larger the crowds the longer Jethmalani talked and the more enthusiastic both he and his audience became. As he entered and left there were shouts of "Victory to the Janata party and victory to Jethmalani!" At three smaller neighborhood meetings, community leaders presented him with garlands of flowers, some of them containing rupee notes, contributions to the campaign.

Since Jethmalani comes originally from the Sind (now in Pakistan) and is unable to speak the local language, Marathi, he generally spoke in Hindi, which most of the Marathi audience could follow. To a predominantly Christian crowd in one neighborhood he spoke first in English and then in Hindi.

In each of his speeches he addressed the issues of freedom and democracy.[1] He denounced Sanjay Gandhi's statement that the country

---

[1] Quotations are from the author's notes.

needed bread not elections and decried the view that only the educated were concerned about freedom. Tens of thousands of people, he said, had come to hear Jayaprakash Narayan and Morarji speak not about economic issues but about democracy, liberty, and arrest without trial. "Without freedom," he said, "the government was able to enforce a compulsory family planning program against the poor. Without freedom the government was bulldozing the homes of slum dwellers. Without freedom workers could not strike for their just demands. Without freedom the Muslim and Christian minorities could not be protected. Only under the rule of law," he said, "could they all be free." Jethmalani charged Gokhale with responsibility for the constitutional amendments that had weakened the power of the courts. Speaking at a meeting of lawyers in central Bombay, Jethmalani alluded to the attacks against Mrs. Gandhi by her aunt, Vijayalakshmi Pandit. He told the lawyers, "As Mrs. Gandhi is a discard of her family, so Mr. Gokhale must be a discard of the lawyers."

At the same meeting M. C. Chagla, a distinguished elderly judge who had once been ambassador to the United States and who was now campaigning for Janata, said that the choice was between democracy and dictatorship and that the rule of law was essential if there were to be liberty. Chagla denounced Mrs. Gandhi for her claim that she, "like Louis XIV," had to remain in power if there were to be a stable government. "Indira is not India and India is not Indira," he said, reversing a much publicized statement made by Dev Kanta Borooah, president of the Congress party. In a democracy, he said, no one is indispensable. He spoke of the lawyers as the vanguard of the freedom struggle. "Gandhi, Motilal, Jawaharlal, and Vallabahi Patel were all lawyers who understood the importance of law in a free society. It is too bad that Mrs. Gandhi is not a lawyer too for perhaps if she were she might have respect for the law." Mrs. Gandhi claimed that she was continuing the emergency in order to assure "stability and progress" for the country, but the only ground provided by the Constitution for maintaining an emergency, Chagla said, was to deal with an internal or external threat to the country's security. As to whether the Janata party had a program for the country, he replied: "What greater program can a party have than the restoration of democracy!"

In addition to the lawyers who canvassed on Jethmalani's behalf and helped fund his campaign, Jethmalani had the support of one of the state's popular Marathi writers, who told an enthusiastic audience that he had come to speak to them for only one reason—to say that they must remove Gokhale as the man responsible for writing the amendments to the Constitution that had deprived them of their freedom. Then he told the laughing audience that he had recently walked into a Bombay bookstore to ask for a copy of the Indian Constitution that had been amended so often by the government and was told by the shopkeeper that he never stocked periodicals!

3

The Government's Excesses

The major issue of the campaign was the emergency. Beyond the arrests and the suppression of freedom, this meant a host of controversial measures and tactics that the opposition denounced and that the government alternately defended, denied, and excused as the "excesses" of an overzealous few. These included the compulsory sterilizations that took place under the government's family planning program, the eviction of thousands of poor people from their homes in the name of slum clearing, and a variety of high-handed acts and cases of intervention in state and local affairs that aroused intense opposition.

The Sterilization Issue

Nasbandi—the Hindi word for vasectomy—was the focus of the campaigning in the Hindi-speaking states of northern India. Neither the vasectomy program nor family planning was new to India during the emergency. What was new was the intensity of the effort and the form the program took.

India was among the earliest of the developing countries to initiate an intensive family planning program. After a variety of experiments, the Indian government launched a campaign for the use of intrauterine devices in 1966. The program did well initially, but then the acceptance rate declined. In an effort to accelerate family planning the government launched a new program in 1971, involving the use of mobile field hospitals or vasectomy camps. The impact of this program was also modest. India's fertility rate was declining, but not as rapidly as many of the planners had hoped. In early 1976 the government made a series of decisions to intensify the vasectomy program by mobilizing the general administrative cadres of state and local authorities, not simply the personnel of the health services, by assigning monthly performance quotas, by providing financial inducements to contraceptive acceptors and to the family planning field staff, and by creating disincentives for central government employees.[1]

The decision to aggressively pursue the vasectomy program was a political one. It was not part of Mrs. Gandhi's Twenty-Point Program, but it was included in Sanjay Gandhi's Five-Point Program. Precisely why Sanjay gave so much importance to the family planning program is unknown: Was it because of a genuine concern for reducing India's high fertility rate? Part of his search for a program that would be distinctively his own? A way of demonstrating to Congressmen, administrators, and the country's middle classes that he was a leader capable of getting things done? A way of exercising control over state politicians and administrators? Perhaps all of these.

Since Sanjay's personal influence was great in the Delhi municipal corporation, it was in the capital city that his new aggressive vasectomy effort was initially launched. But as the emergency progressed, Sanjay's influence soon extended outside of Delhi, and senior government officials, cabinet members, and the prime minister herself urged visiting chief ministers to consult with Sanjay on a variety of state concerns. Sanjay worked closely with Bansi Lal, former chief minister of Haryana, minister of defense, and a member of Mrs. Gandhi's inner group of close advisors. Sanjay's and Bansi Lal's influence was particularly great on the chief ministers of the Hindi-speaking states.[2] It was these state governments that adopted vasectomy quotas and created traveling vasectomy camps that moved from village to village to ensure that the quotas were met.

Quotas were imposed on individual state and local government officials. "There is hardly a school teacher, a civil servant, railwayman or police inspector in this sprawling state," wrote one observer, "whose pay, promotion, or confirmation was not held up pending the production by him or her of certificates to show that he or she had motivated a requisite number of persons to undergo sterilization."[3]

---

[1] As a disincentive, the government decided that central government employees with more than three children would not be eligible for government accommodations and loans for building houses until they produced sterilization certificates. The disincentives were dropped on March 5, 1977. See *Times of India*, March 6, 1977.

[2] Their influence was not so great in the non-Hindi states. Tamil Nadu and Gujarat were controlled by opposition parties in the early months of the emergency, then placed under the administrative control of the central government. In Kerala, Congress shared power with other parties. In Kashmir, Sheikh Abdullah, the chief minister, was politically secure. Moreover, most of the members of Mrs. Gandhi's inner group came from the Hindi-speaking states.

[3] Inder Malhotra, "Congress Worse Off in U.P. than Bihar," *Times of India*, March 4, 1977.

The result was that officials often forced local people to undergo sterilization. Given the generally poor quality of the administration in many of the north Indian states and the speed with which the vasectomy camps moved from village to village, it is not surprising that some of the vasectomies were performed under unsanitary conditions. Stories of forcible sterilization of the young, accounts of villagers' fleeing into the fields at night to escape the surgical knife, of postoperative infections and even deaths rapidly spread through the countryside during the emergency. And since government workers attempting to fulfill their quotas were reluctant to coerce the rich and educated, it was generally the lowest classes who were pulled into the vasectomy camps.[4]

During the election campaign, the press regularly reported accounts of forced vasectomies:

> Among the victims are a forty-five year old Muslim and his younger brother who was forced to undergo sterilization last November. The circumstances in which the incidents took place make it even more tragic. Their mother had just died and they had gone to the town to purchase a piece of white cloth to cover the coffin. A couple of policemen dragged them into a jeep and took them to the health center where they were forcibly sterilized despite protests and tearful pleas.[5]

Or again:

> A sixty-five year old Harijan widow sat next to this reporter in a Gohana-bound bus. She was going to meet her daughter, married to a municipal sweeper. When asked if she knew the elections to the Lok Sabha were around the corner, she

[4] On March 17 a report was issued to the press on a survey conducted by Professor D. Banerji of Jawaharlal Nehru University on the government's family planning program. Field investigators spent about a week each in villages in Gujarat, Karnataka, Rajasthan, Tamil Nadu, Uttar Pradesh, and West Bengal between October 1976 and January 1977. According to the survey there was widespread use of police raids and physical force to procure sterilization cases and in several states the entire government machinery under the leadership of the local deputy commissioner of the district was mobilized to exert pressure on people to be sterilized. Professor Banerji said that the issuing of licenses for guns, shops, cane crushers, and vehicles, grants of loans, registration of land, the issuing of ration cards, exemption from payment of school fees or land taxes, supply of canal water, and any form of registration appointments, transfers, bail applications, or facilities relating to court cases were linked with the procurement of cases for sterilization. He said that villages which put up resistance to the sterilization campaign were raided by sterilization personnel and police. There were instances, he said, when almost the entire adult population of the village fled to the fields at the sight of approaching vehicles. The survey reported that the "weaker sections," a phrase generally referring to Harijans and minorities, usually formed the focus of the raids. (*Times of India*, March 17, 1977.)

[5] Ibid., March 6, 1977.

said: "Babuji, you will see what this lady gets this time! She had rendered my four sons and three sons-in-law impotent." Her neighbor had hid her sons in a sugar cane field for some time. "It was their bad luck" she sighed, "that they were caught after a few days and were sterilized."[6]

Some of the most intense opposition to the vasectomy campaign came from the Muslims. Among the least educated groups in India and one of the poorest, the Muslims have by and large continued to have large families. Pressed by local officials to undergo sterilizations, Muslims sometimes resisted by force. In a particularly nasty incident between the police and the Muslims at Turkman Gate in old Delhi, a number of Muslims were killed.[7] Word of the Turkman Gate incident, which came to symbolize the government's forced sterilization program, spread to Muslim communities throughout northern India.

Popular hostility to the compulsory sterilization program was so great that one life-long Congressman said: "These damned vasectomies have become something like the greased cartridges of 1857."[8] After completing a tour of several north Indian states, Inder Malhotra, an editor for the *Times of India,* predicted that Congress would do badly in the states of Uttar Pradesh, Punjab, Bihar, Haryana, and Himachal where Bansi Lal and Sanjay had been most influential in pressing for the sterilization program.[9] Since Muslims, Harijans, and other low-income communities were hit hardest by the government quotas, Malhotra anticipated that these groups would vote against the government. He thought that local officials in these states would also turn against the government, not because they objected to the quotas, but because the government was now blaming them for some of the "excesses" of the emergency. "The officials," he wrote, "resent being used as a scapegoat for the government's excesses."[10]

On March 5 a statement was issued by the All India State Government Employees Federation rebuking the government for its attempt to blame its employees for the excesses of the family planning program. The statement said that the state governments were responsible

---

[6] Ibid.

[7] For an eyewitness account of the incident at Turkman Gate, see Jawid Laiq, "The Day Recalled," *Indian Express,* April 19, 1977, reprinted in *Seminar,* June 1977, pp. 20–22.

[8] Malhotra, "Congress Worse Off." The 1857 mutiny of Muslim troops against their British officers was reportedly precipitated by rumors that the cartridges of bullets were greased with pork lard, a practice offensive to Muslims.

[9] Ibid. The prediction proved to be accurate. Congress declined by twenty-three percentage points in Uttar Pradesh and by seventeen in Bihar.

[10] For another account of the hostility of the bureaucracy to vasectomy quotas, see "Officials Feel They Have Been Made Scapegoats," *Indian Express,* March 15, 1977.

in that they had established quotas as a means of motivating people to participate.

> When employees could not achieve the quota, it resulted in withholding their increments, recovery of double the house rent due, non-drawal of salaries, and even discharge from service. For example, in Bihar alone, over 600 employees lost their jobs and 50,000 were not given their salaries for three months. . . . The terror-stricken employees were literally driven to fall on the hapless people.

Moreover, according to the statement, the chief ministers and health ministers of the states had drawn up targets for sterilization and even "coerced government employees to undergo sterilization." It was preposterous for those in power to assume an air of "injured innocence and pretend ignorance of all that was going on under their very nose. . . . Those who drive a wedge between the employees and the people do not serve the real interests of the nation. They serve only themselves."[11]

Slum Clearance and the Muslim Reaction

The beautification of Delhi was another of Sanjay Gandhi's pet projects. Sanjay persuaded the Delhi municipal corporation and the Delhi Development Authority (which has primary responsibility for urban planning) to improve the city by clearing shops and huts that had encroached on public spaces. The first structures to be leveled were the huts that had been built by Muslim squatters on the public spaces around Jama Masjid, the largest mosque in India. Subsequently, many of their inhabitants were transported to locations ten to fifteen miles from the city. Although eventually many of the slum dwellers were provided with new housing, there was widespread anger at the summary manner in which the government had bulldozed their dwellings and transported them to areas far from where most of them worked.[12]

As many as 150,000 structures were demolished in Delhi, 137,000 of them by the Delhi Development Authority, nearly 11,000 by the Delhi Corporation, and 1,400 by the New Delhi Municipal Committee.[13] Demolitions took place initially at Jama Masjid and at Turkman

---

[11] *Times of India*, March 6, 1977.

[12] The *Indian Express* reported (March 3, 1977) that slum dwellers were often obliged to have themselves sterilized to obtain housing sites.

[13] These figures are from testimony presented before the Shah Commission in December 1977. The Delhi municipal commissioner told the commission that "Sanjay Gandhi was the de facto administrator of the municipal corporation of Delhi," and the minister for works and housing said that the demolitions took place without his approval. See the *Overseas Hindustan Times*, December 22, 1977.

Gate, both Muslim quarters, and subsequently in the Karol Bagh area, a predominantly Hindu section of the city where the Jana Sangh had considerable political support.[14]

While Janata candidates made much of the demolition program in their campaign speeches, the greatest hostility came from some of the Muslim opponents of the government. Perhaps the most outspoken Muslim critic was Hazrat Abdullah Shah Bukhari, the Imam or religious leader of Jama Masjid. An imposing bearded figure in long robes, the Imam had incurred the wrath of the authorities during the emergency by speaking out against the slum clearing program in Delhi.

Muslims constitute 11.2 percent of the population of India—61,400,000 out of a population of 548,000,000 in 1971. There are Muslim concentrations in Kashmir (where Muslims form a majority), Uttar Pradesh, Bihar, Kerala, Maharashtra, West Bengal, and Andhra. In earlier elections, the Muslims had tended to vote for the Congress party, but it was clear that in this election campaign a large portion of the Muslim electorate had turned against the government. The sterilization program and the demolitions seemed to be significant reasons.

During the campaign, the Imam regularly toured predominantly Muslim areas all over the country, presenting his case against the government. On March 13, he spoke at a crowded press conference at the Sarovar Hotel in Hyderabad before going off to address a large crowd at a public meeting. Speaking in his booming voice, the Imam accused Mrs. Gandhi's government of turning Indian Muslims against the Jana Sangh and the RSS, the militant Hindu youth organization. He said that the attacks against these Hindu groups were part of the government's effort to follow the old British policy of divide and rule. The Imam surprised his audiences by saying that he did not believe that the RSS or the Jana Sangh was anti-Muslim, and he called upon the government to end its ban on the RSS, whose political workers were still in jail. "It is not the RSS or the Jana Sangh," he said,

> that fired on Muslims at Turkman Gate, but the government. It was not the RSS and Jana Sangh that introduced coercion into family planning, but the government. It was not the RSS and the Jana Sangh that used bulldozers against Muslims near Jama Masjid, but the government. It was not the Jana Sangh and the RSS that arrested Muslim opponents of the government and banned the Jammaat-e-Islami, it was the government.

---

[14] "This is a Jana Sangh market. Pull this down," Sanjay is reported to have commanded civil officials when he visited the Gaffar Market in Karol Bagh on August 8, 1975. Two days later the market was torn down. *Overseas Hindustan Times*, December 22, 1977.

Finally, he said, it was not the Jana Sangh or the RSS that had arrested him, but the government. "Freedom for the Muslims," he concluded, "depends not upon the election of a pro-Muslim government, but on living in a country in which the laws protect all communities."[15]

The Imam chose to cast the sufferings of Muslims not as a sectarian issue but as another instance of a kind of oppression that cut across caste, class, and religious lines. He did so at a time when some of the groups that had previously been regarded as anti-Muslim were equally willing to rise above religious differences. The Jana Sangh, in particular, with its strong Hindu nationalist orientation, made deliberate efforts to dispel its sectarian image during the campaign.

Party representatives denied that the Jana Sangh favored the assimilation of Muslims into Hindu society and asserted that they recognized the rights of Muslims to retain a separate religion and culture. They denied that the Jana Sangh or the RSS was responsible for the Hindu-Muslim riots that had occurred in various parts of the country since independence. In the areas of India where Jana Sangh was strongest, they said, there had not been sectarian riots. The Jana Sangh had even nominated Muslims for state assembly and parliamentary constituencies. As one Jana Sangh politician explained to the author, "Let Muslim workers make demands as workers and Muslim slum dwellers make demands as slum dwellers. What we oppose is the demand for exclusive rights for Muslims alone."

"Acts of Highhandedness"

The efforts of Indira and Sanjay Gandhi to bring the Congress party organization in Bombay under close central control have already been described. Other instances of government meddling in local affairs abounded.

Events in the northern state of Haryana, home of Sanjay's ally Bansi Lal, were a case in point. Bansi Lal's constituency, Dhiwani, was generally considered a Congress stronghold and had been nursed so well over the years that some observers thought the seat might not be contested by the opposition. Bansi Lal was widely regarded as an able chief minister who had played a significant role in accelerating economic development in the state and had been particularly conscientious about assisting his constituents. But reporters touring the constituency during the campaign described anger against Bansi Lal and the Congress party government. "Residents of village after village refer to acts of highhandedness, not all of them connected with family

---

[15]From the author's notes at the press conference. A summary of his remarks appears in the *Deccan Chronicle*, March 14, 1977.

planning," wrote the correspondent for the *Times of India*.[16] In particular, many influential village leaders who had been elected to local bodies or cooperative societies had been replaced by their defeated rivals, appointed by the government. The reporter noted that there was universal opposition to the appointment of leaders of local bodies. "If the fate of a *sarpanch* [local government representative] is to be decided by someone in Chandigarh or New Delhi," said a former village schoolteacher, "we must then have our own man to wield power in Chandigarh or New Delhi." This, the reporter went on to say, explained the keen interest of villagers in the elections. One of the parliamentary candidates was reported to have said, "Villagers are taking as much interest in the Lok Sabha elections this time as they generally do in elections to the village *panchayats*."[17] In Haryana, Janata would take 70.4 percent of the vote.

Throughout northern India there had been indiscriminate political arrests immediately after the emergency was declared. While no official figures were released, the opposition claimed that thousands of arrests had taken place in each of the larger states. In Madhya Pradesh alone, the opposition claimed, as many as 17,000 persons were in prison.[18] In Madhya Pradesh it was also reported that some 4,000 government employees and officials had been dismissed from the government on grounds of inefficiency and corruption, but many of the dismissals, it was charged, were actually political.[19] Target setting —for arrests, dismissals, sterilizations—seemed to be a regular feature of the emergency in Madhya Pradesh. According to official statistics, a million sterilizations were performed in a few months against the annual target of 267,000.[20]

---

[16] *Times of India*, March 4, 1977.

[17] Turnout in India (unlike that in the United States) is ordinarily higher in local and state elections than in national parliamentary elections.

[18] This and other estimates of political arrests made during the election campaign were exaggerated. According to the Shah Commission, the number of persons detained throughout India during the emergency totaled 36,039. The largest number of arrests were in Uttar Pradesh (7,049), Madhya Pradesh (6,212), Maharashtra (5,475), West Bengal (5,320), and Bihar (2,360). It is worth noting that less than 10 percent of all the arrests (3,428) were in south India. The figures cover the period from June 25, 1975, through March 19, 1977. *Overseas Hindustan Times*, December 22, 1977.

[19] V. T. Joshi, "The Congress in a Daze—What Happened in Madhya Pradesh," *Times of India*, April 2, 1977.

[20] Detailed figures on the vasectomy program have been pulled together from a variety of government sources by Davidson R. Gwatkin of the Overseas Development Council in a draft manuscript, "India's Emergency Family Planning Effort: The Importance of Political Will Reconsidered," October 1977. According to Gwatkin, 8,100,000 people were sterilized during 1976–1977, 6,500,000 of them during the six months from July through December 1976.

And throughout the north such policies mobilized and unified the opposition. "A happy feature of the polling this time in Madhya Pradesh," wrote one reporter after the election, was that "factors like caste and communal barriers and day-to-day economic hardships were ignored by most people, whose main concern was to defeat the hated emergency regime."[21] The large sums of money spent by Congress in many constituencies apparently did not have any effect on the voters. Rightly or wrongly they were convinced that Mrs. Gandhi wanted to stick to power at any cost and to entrench her son. Rickshaw drivers and bus conductors talked of the "contrived" emergence of Sanjay Gandhi with the help of what they called "hired crowds" during the emergency. It was in Madhya Pradesh that Sanjay delivered a speech reported all over India. Addressing a crowd of about 8,000 people, Sanjay described those who supported the Janata party as traitors. When he asked how many such traitors were present only three hands were raised. But he persisted in attacking the Janata "traitors" and again challenged the "traitors" to identify themselves. At that point almost the entire crowd raised its hands and kept them raised until Sanjay left in a huff.[22]

During the campaign it was expected that Bihar would be a disaster area for the Congress party. Congress had won only 40 percent of the vote in Bihar at the height of the "Indira wave" and it was generally regarded as having lost that support even before the emergency was declared. It was in Bihar that Jayaprakash Narayan had launched his movement for "total revolution" against corrupt ministers and administrators in 1974. The Bihar movement was, as one analyst put it, an upsurge of the urban middle class, who resented inflation, urban unemployment, food shortages, and governmental corruption.[23] Reports coming out of Bihar during the election campaign suggested that opposition to the government had spread from the urban middle classes to other social classes, each with its particular grievance: industrial workers and coal miners resented the termination of bonuses; small traders and shopkeepers, government harassment; farmers, the rising costs of agricultural imports; school teachers in the countryside, the way they were forced to bring "cases" for *nasbandi*; agricultural laborers, the fact that they did not receive the enhanced wages promised by the government. Before such grievances, caste as well as class differences seemed to disappear. As one journalist wrote a few days after the returns were in, "Voters did not

[21] Joshi, "Congress in a Daze."

[22] *Indian Express*, March 11, 1977.

[23] Ghanshyam Shah, "Revolution, Reform, or Protest?" *Economic and Political Weekly*, April 16, 1977.

bother in the least whether the candidate they were voting for was a Kayastha or a Maithili Brahmin, a Bhumihar or a Rajput, a Harijan or a Kurmi. Their main aim was to get rid of the emergency regime."[24]

Even in the south, where the Congress party would do well, the government's autocratic policies were an issue. One of the few people the author met in Andhra who had defected from the Congress party to the Janata party was a member of the faculty at Osmania University in Hyderabad. He complained that the government had suspended elections for village and district councils (*panchayat samithis* and *zilla parishads*) and municipal corporations, and that special officers had been appointed to take charge of all of the local governments in Andhra. The result, he said, was that officials had become all-powerful throughout the state; the land reform legislation had not helped the landless but had simply enriched the members of the revenue department. "If you want to get anything done," he said,

> now you must deal with a government of officials. We would rather deal with corrupt politicians than with corrupt officials. A politician must be concerned with my feelings since he wants my votes but the bureaucrat knows that eventually he will be transfererd to another district. Besides, the official always has his pension! Once the politicians in this state used to have influence here because of their feudal authority, but because of elections their power came to rest upon the services they provide to local people. But since the politicians no longer have any influence, we must now deal directly with corrupt officials.
>
> Under the emergency, the Congress party has broken down. There have been no elections to party posts in years. Everything is done by nominations. Even our chief minister was appointed by New Delhi. Now some unknown person has been chosen as president of the Andhra Pradesh Congress Committee. We are supposed to follow him. A lot of Congress politicians here feel that they would be holding posts in the party or in the government if there had been elections. Ambitions have been frustrated because there has been no intra-party democracy.

The author asked a high official in the Andhra state government how true these charges were, and his response shed further light on the government's methods. He agreed that the suspension of local government had weakened the rural base of the Congress party and that there was much opposition to the chief minister of the state, particularly on the part of the members of the Reddy caste,

[24] Subhash Kirpekar, "Caste Factor Was of No Account—Bihar Poll Sea Change," *Times of India*, April 5, 1977.

most of whom were supporters of Brahmananda Reddy, the home minister in Mrs. Ganhdi's cabinet. Within the Congress party Reddy was widely regarded as a potential defector, not because he objected on principle to the emergency but because he had been humiliated by Indira Gandhi's appointment of one of her closest supporters as his deputy in the home ministry. A tactical move on the part of the prime minister, this was designed to maintain her effective control over a minister whose loyalty she questioned. Not only the home minister, but also the finance minister was kept in tow this way. Ironically, these two were among the few ministers who were not defeated in the elections. Some observers attributed their success to the fact that their deputies, and not they, were held responsible for the excesses committed by the two ministries.

Two professional groups that were alarmed by the government's methods were businessmen and lawyers. The industrialists had initially welcomed the emergency as a means of restoring order and discipline; they particularly approved of the ban on strikes, restrictions on bonuses for workers, the lower tax rates on higher incomes, the relaxation of government controls over business, the new emphasis on export promotion, and a variety of right-of-center economic policies. But later many members of the business community became fearful of Indira Gandhi and of Sanjay. There were income tax investigations of several well-known industrialists and even raids upon their homes. Many businessmen became concerned at what they felt was neither left-wing nor right-wing government, but arbitrary government, with a few individuals, Sanjay and Bansi Lal above all, exercising arbitrary power.

One Calcutta businessman, an executive with Tata Steel, expressed the hope that the Congress party would win, but by a reduced majority so that some of the excessive features of the emergency might be dropped. This now appeared to be typical of the business community. The worst outcome, he said, would be a Janata victory because "that would mean unstable government." The opposition, he believed, was bound to fall apart when it was no longer a simple matter of opposing Indira Gandhi but time to hammer out tax policies or import-export policies or budget priorities.[25]

Among lawyers there was bitter opposition to the constitutional amendments and Mrs. Gandhi's efforts to place herself above the law. One Calcutta lawyer, a one-time Socialist who for the last fifteen years had not actively taken part in politics, told the author that he was devoting all his time to campaigning for the Janata candidate in his constituency. "If Janata wins," he said, "we hope

[25] Interview with the author.

there will be a commission of inquiry for Sanjay and possibly for Mrs. Gandhi as well. . . . Can you imagine that lawyers should be marching in public demonstrations in the streets of Calcutta?" Not only were they angry at the government's suspension of civil liberties and at its efforts to destroy the independence of the judiciary, but also they were aroused at the government's efforts to get control of the national bar association. In West Bengal, according to this informant, the bar councils were now actively working against the Congress party in all of the district towns throughout the state.

By the end of the campaign it was clear that the measures that had been adopted by Mrs. Gandhi's government during the emergency had alienated one constituency after another. The sterilization program had generated powerful fears among all social classes in northern India, especially the Harijans and the Muslims. The elimination of the compulsory bonus system, a popular policy that had actually been supported by Mrs. Gandhi years before to ensure increased income for industrial workers regardless of a firm's productivity or profits, had alienated industrial labor. The compulsory deposit scheme, under which a portion of the annual increments of wage earners were put into compulsory savings certificates, had antagonized the middle as well as the working classes. Shopkeepers, at first irritated by the government's insistence that fixed prices be marked on all items for sale, had come to fear police harassment. Landlord moneylenders disliked the government's announcement that rural debts would be abolished; nor did the announcement win the hearts and minds of peasants, who quickly recognized that in the absence of alternative credit sources they would remain dependent on local moneylenders. The legal profession was angry at the suspension of the rule of law, the transfer and dismissal of judges for political reasons, and the arrest of lawyers who opposed the government. Journalists were equally angry at the suspension of a free press, the intrusion of the ministry of information into the internal management of the newspapers and wire services, and the arrest of fellow journalists.

Above all, the emergency had created a system of arbitrary government by arbitrary men. Many a rural community and urban neighborhood had its little Sanjay. Politicians, government officials, landlords, and local toughs, usually members of Sanjay's Youth Congress, had used their connections to push people around. Sanjay and his three closest allies, Bansi Lal, Om Mehta, and Vidhya Charan Shukla (some Indians called them the "gang of four"), had created an atmosphere of total mistrust of government in the Hindi-speaking states. Whether or not the most alarming reports of compulsory sterilization, arrests, and police excesses were exaggerated, fear had spread through northern India.

Mrs. Gandhi and her closest supporters, including Sanjay himself, had alternated between denying these reports, asserting that there had been a few excesses of which the reports were exaggerated, and casting blame upon "overzealous" state and local officials. This last charge, as we have noted, proved to be a political liability. Government officials reacted vehemently, insisting that responsibility rested with the government leaders who had given the bureaucracy its orders.

Janata party candidates campaigned on a single issue: restoring democracy. Economic issues were secondary, except insofar as they illustrated the problems that arose when individuals were deprived of their right to protest. A certain moral aura surrounded many of the Janata parliamentary candidates. The arrest of Jayaprakash Narayan, a man who had never held and did not seek public office and who was widely regarded as a moral leader in India—part of what the British political scientist W. H. Morris-Jones describes as India's "saintly tradition"—struck many Indians as an obviously disreputable act. It threw a kind of moral blanket over all the political arrests that followed.

Janata candidates pointed out that arrests had been made by the government without written charges. Again and again they cited the statement made by the solicitor general that during the emergency government officials had the right to arrest an individual, imprison him, and even shoot him without recourse to the courts. It is noteworthy that one of the largest margins of victory would go to George Fernandes, the Socialist leader from Bombay who remained in jail even as he stood for Parliament and who had been accused by the government of collecting arms to violently overthrow the government.

Finally, it should be noted that the government's charge that the Janata leaders had been trying to destroy India's fragile institutions—and after the election that their victory would result in unstable government—fell on deaf ears. The opposition contained too many prominent figures to lend credence to the government's attack. Four of the leading figures in the opposition, Morarji Desai, Jagjivan Ram, H. N. Bahaguna, and Charan Singh, were establishment politicians who had once been at the center of power.

Last-Minute Attempts to Recoup

During the final weeks of the campaign, the Congress party was clearly on the defensive. Prominent Congress leaders stopped touring the country and concentrated on their own constituencies. Sanjay, evidently hearing reports of the mood within his own constituency and discovering that unsympathetic and even hostile audiences greeted him on his tours, devoted the last few weeks almost exclusively to his own campaign. Of the Congress leaders, only Mrs. Gandhi toured widely. In contrast, the opposition had an impressive array of nationally known leaders on tour, providing further force to the argument that Janata had the national leaders capable of governing the country.

As election day approached, many of the state governments in northern India announced special concessions to sections of the electorate. In Uttar Pradesh, the Congress chief minister announced that land revenue taxes would be reduced by 50 percent. The government of Bihar announced that there would be an increase in the dearness (cost-of-living) and medical allowances paid to government employees retroactive to January 1, 1977. The state would also provide free medical care for all those who had taken part in the nationalist movement some thirty years earlier. And an increase was announced in the pay scale of all college teachers, retroactive to January 1973. The government of West Bengal declared that its employees would receive increased rent allowances and medical grants, while the Congress governments in Haryana, Himachal Pradesh, and the Punjab all announced that they too would provide additional dearness allowances to government employees. One journal estimated that these new benefits totaled over $200 million of public funds.[26]

"Whether these concessions will have any major impact on the outcome of the elections it is difficult to foretell," reported the *Economic and Political Weekly*, a well-known Bombay journal. "The majority of India's poor may be illiterate, but they are not dumb. . . . Through these concessions," the editorial went on, "a party which had been talking itself hoarse about the need for economic discipline has openly flaunted its economic irresponsibility. A party which is supposedly wedded to the objective of conserving resources for development is frittering away these resources in order to tilt the scale of electoral fortunes in its favor."[27]

---

[26] *Economic and Political Weekly*, March 5, 1977, p. 409.
[27] Ibid.

4

Regional Patterns

Close-up on Tamil Nadu

Regional peculiarities dominated the campaign in India's southern-most state, Tamil Nadu. A pro-Tamil anti-northern party with roots in an anti-Brahmin movement dating back to the 1920s, the Dravida Munnetra Kazhagam (DMK) dominated the party system here. Secessionist until the early 1960s, the DMK had emerged as the largest opposition party in the state in the 1962 elections. In 1967 it had formed a government in Tamil Nadu, the only state where an opposition party was able to form a government on its own, and this government had remained in power until 1976. In 1969 the DMK had supported Mrs. Gandhi in her fight against the group that split off to form the Congress O., and in 1971 Mrs. Gandhi had returned the favor by not running Congress candidates against the DMK in the simultaneous state assembly and parliamentary elections held that year. The local Congress party, however, had been unhappy with this alliance, which had subsequently fallen apart. During the emergency, the DMK had opposed the central government, and Tamil Nadu had become a center for underground activities. Many of the underground newspapers, most of them mimeographed sheets, that were circulated throughout India originated in Tamil Nadu. Moreover, the DMK had been unwilling to arrest opponents of Mrs. Gandhi. It had come as no surprise, therefore, when early in 1976 the central government had suspended the DMK government and placed the state under president's rule.

Moreover, in Tamil Nadu the 1977 election was for all practical purposes fought between two DMK groups, one led by Muther Karunanidhi, chief minister of the state from 1969 to 1976, which retained the name DMK, and the other led by M. G. Ramachandran, which had split off in 1972 and had taken the name All India "Anna" DMK (AIADMK) after Annadurai, the founder of the DMK. Ramachandran was a film actor and the idol of women and young moviegoers in a state where the film industry is an important social and political force. "MGR," as he was popularly called, accused the DMK of running a corrupt and inefficient state government. There was considerable feeling that the DMK state government was unpopular in spite of its opposition to the emergency.

In Tamil Nadu the two national parties simply took sides in the struggle between the two regional parties. The DMK formed an alliance with the Janata party; the choice was logical given their common hostility to Mrs. Gandhi and the Congress party, yet problematic in that the local Janata party consisted largely of people who had split from the Congress in 1969 and had a long tradition of rivalry with the DMK. Though the crowds at Janata-DMK meetings were large, many observers felt that the emergency would be a secondary issue here.

Since the DMK and the Janata party were allied, it made political sense for Ramachandran's party to ally itself with Congress. Some thought that if the Congress party won in Tamil Nadu it would be largely because of the unpopularity of the DMK and the personal popularity of Ramachandran, who specialized in playing clean-cut, incorruptible heroes on the screen.

The outcome of the election was a victory for the AIADMK and its Congress ally: the AIADMK won nearly half of the parliamentary seats in the state—eighteen out of thirty-nine—while Congress picked up fourteen seats. At the state level, it was a victory for the opposition since a vote for either Congress or the AIADMK could be seen as a vote against the DMK state government. Apparently state rather than national issues and personalities were decisive in Tamil Nadu. A few days after the poll one south Indian commentator wrote:

> The fact remains that, though hundreds of thousands of people in Tamil Nadu turned up at the scores of public meetings at all hours of day and night, the excesses which caused deep revulsion against the Congress in the North did not influence the voting patterns in the South in the least. The reason is that the cases of gross abuse of emergency powers were confined largely to the states north of the Vindhyas. The emergency measures were enforced in the South much less ruthlessly. During the seven months of the emergency it was in power, the DMK government used the extraordinary powers in a limited way for its own purposes vis-à-vis political opponents. . . . When President's rule

was established in Tamil Nadu at the end of January 1976, the authorities did arrest several thousand political workers, largely DMK men. But most of them were released within the year. . . . The main issue in Tamil Nadu was clearly the fact of institutionalized corruption under DMK regime. . . . Try however it might to explain its decision the Janata party blundered grievously in allying itself with the DMK.[1]

The Communists and the Campaign in West Bengal

Only two national opposition parties refused to join Janata: the Communist party of India (CPI) and the Communist party Marxist (CPM) which had split off from the CPI in 1964. These two parties had won twenty-three and twenty-five seats respectively in the 1971 parliamentary elections, with 4.7 and 5.1 percent of the vote. Both had their main strength in two states at opposite ends of India, West Bengal and Kerala, where they fought against one another and where both had participated in governments at various times.[2]

Kerala had had a CPM government from 1967 to 1969, when it was ousted by a coalition of the CPI and Congress, the first such ever to form a state government. In West Bengal the CPM had won 18.1 percent of the vote—nearly three times as much as the CPI (6.8 percent)—in the 1967 state elections. However, the two parties had joined together, along with other opposition parties, to form a united front government in West Bengal for a few months in 1967 and again from February 1969 to April 1970, when president's rule was established. In the West Bengal state assembly elections of 1971, the CPM vote had soared to 33.8 percent, for the first time surpassing the Congress vote (29.8 percent), while the CPI had won only 8.7 percent of the vote.[3] With no one able to form a stable government in the state, elections had again been held the following year. This time there had been a decline in the vote for both Communist parties, though the CPI, which allied itself with Congress, had increased its share of seats in the assembly.

The two parties took diametrically opposed stands toward the

---

[1] V. G. Prasado Rao, "Why No Tremor in the South?" *Times of India*, March 29, 1977.

[2] For an analysis of the regional roots of the Communist movement in India, see Paul R. Brass and Marcus F. Franda, eds., *Radical Politics in South Asia* (Cambridge: MIT Press, 1973).

[3] For an analysis of the 1971 elections in West Bengal, see Marcus F. Franda, *Radical Politics in West Bengal* (Cambridge: MIT Press, 1971), pp. 270–279; and Myron Weiner and John Osgood Field, eds., *Electoral Politics in the Indian States*, vol. 1, *The Communist Parties of West Bengal*, by John Osgood Field and Marcus F. Franda (New Delhi: Manohar Book Service, 1974).

emergency. The CPM had always rejected CPI's willingness to work with Congress, which it regarded as a reactionary party of the big bourgeoisie, and advocated instead a united front from below of workers and peasants on the Chinese model. Militantly opposed to the Congress party, the CPM consistently denounced the emergency and was itself one of the earliest victims of arrests in West Bengal even before the emergency was declared. In the 1977 election the CPM supported Janata.

The pro-Soviet CPI, which had long advocated alliance with what it considered the progressive elements of the nationalist bourgeoisie— that is, the left-of-center pro-Soviet wing of the Congress party— had supported Indira Gandhi ever since the 1969 split within the Congress. It was the only significant non-Congress party that welcomed the emergency, the arrest of opposition leaders, the banning of political organizations, and restrictions on the "capitalist" press.[4] But within a few months it became apparent that the Communists too were feeling the brunt of the repressive measures. Strikes were illegal, the automatic annual bonuses to workers had been ended, and public meetings of trade unions were prohibited, all of which angered many of the Communist rank and file, especially in the trade union movement.

The emergence of Sanjay also alarmed the Communists. Sanjay's public attack on the Communists, his antisocialist probusiness attitudes, and his efforts to build a mass-based militant Youth Congress seemed to them to push the country in a reactionary, if not fascistic, direction. A few months before the elections Sanjay succeeded in deposing the left-of-center chief minister of the state of Orissa, Nandini Satpathy, who had once been a member of the Communist party. In response, the CPI launched a frontal attack on what it described euphemistically as "extraconstitutional forces" and tried to drive a wedge between Mrs. Gandhi, whom it continued to support, and Sanjay. Much to their surprise, no doubt, Mrs. Gandhi herself responded with a series of speeches accusing the Communists of being antinational and reminding the country of their opposition to the nationalist movement and support for the British during the Second World War. In a very personal speech she attacked those who

---

[4] The position of the Communist party on the emergency can be found in the following party publications: C. Rajeswara Rao, Bhupesh Gupta, and Mohit Sen, *Emergency and the Communist Party*, August 1975; N. K. Krishnan, Raj Bahadur Gour, and T. N. Siddhanta, *Working Class and the Emergency*, August 1975; *Report and Resolutions Adopted by the National Council of the Communist Party of India*, Trivandrum, February 1976; and *Report and Resolutions of the Central Executive Committee of the Communist Party of India*, New Delhi, October 1976.

tried to draw a line between herself and her son and talked about the way in which the Nehru family would rally to defend itself.

When the elections were called the central committee of the CPI announced that it would support the Congress but that it would permit each of the state Communist parties to decide whether to work with the government or with the opposition. In West Bengal the CPI supported Congress, but in Bihar and Uttar Pradesh it sided with the opposition. The absurdity of the Communist position was captured by a cartoon in the *Hindustan Times*: a man at a microphone asks a crowd of people, "All those for Congress raise their hands," and then, "Those for Janata. . . ." After the count he turns to a spectacled member of the crowd and asks: "How is it you raise one hand for Congress and the other for Janata?" The reply: "I'm CPI."

In public meetings opposition candidates ridiculed the Communists, saying that the CPI urged people to "vote for the cow without the calf." As one observer wrote, the CPI trade union leader's "infamous statement—the workers have to suffer the travails of the emergency, including a reduction in their living standards, so that Mrs. Gandhi could smash right reaction—haunted the CPI cadres as they went round scrounging for precious electoral support."[5]

West Bengal was one of the few states where there was genuine concern over the possibility of rigging since it was generally agreed that in the 1971 parliamentary elections there had been massive rigging by Congress party workers and local officials to prevent a victory of the Communist party Marxist. Even then, the CPM had won twenty out of the state's forty parliamentary seats in 1971, as against thirteen for Congress. The morning after the 1977 polling, the press reported ballot stuffing in several constituencies and there were authenticated charges that duplicate ballots had been printed. Some of the Janata organizers feared that the rigging might have cost them several seats in the city. The Election Commission provided considerable reassurance—not only for West Bengal but for the entire country—when it announced that there would be a repolling in a number of the polling stations the next day.[6]

If there was any rigging by the Congress party it hardly affected the outcome of the elections in West Bengal since Congress won only three of the state's forty-two seats. The results here were

---

[5] Ashok Mitra, "The State of the Left," *Times of India*, March 29, 1977.

[6] Polling throughout India proved to be peaceful and, contrary to what had happened just a week earlier in Pakistan's national parliamentary elections, there were few instances of poll rigging. The reports of rigging in Pakistan, however, made Janata politicians acutely concerned over the possibility of similar occurrences in India.

a surprise, even to Janata leaders, who, though they had expected Congress to lose, had feared that it would retain nearly half of the state's parliamentary delegation. One reason for their pessimism was that the Congress government of the state, under the chief minister- ship of Siddharta Shankar Ray, had survived an attempt by Sanjay Gandhi to replace the chief minister with someone more susceptible to his influence. Siddharta Ray was generally regarded as one of the earliest supporters of the emergency and he was widely held re- sponsible for the massive arrests that had taken place in West Bengal. But his clash with Mrs. Gandhi over Sanjay, many thought, had given him some political points that might win him support with the electorate. Sanjay himself had failed to get control of the Youth Congress organization in West Bengal, which remained under the leadership of Priya Das Munshi, a bright, tough, ambitious young anti-Communist politician who was standing for Parliament.

Nonetheless, the opposition parties swept the state and carried all the seats in Calcutta. The seats were evenly divided, sixteen to the Janata party, sixteen to their ally, the Communist party Marxist, and two to minor parties. The Communist party of India was wiped out.

Other Regional Parties

There were a few other regional parties of some importance in 1977. The Shiromani Akali Dal was first organized in the 1920s as a re- form movement within the Sikh community, a religious group that broke from Hinduism in the sixteenth century and is now concen- trated in the Punjab. In 1947 the Akali Dal had called for the crea- tion of a separate Sikh state independent of both India and Pakistan, and in the 1950s it had called for the creation of a Sikh-majority Punjabi-speaking state within the Indian union. The Akalis had per- sisted in their demand until 1966 when the central government agreed to partition the Punjab to create a predominantly Sikh state retaining the name Punjab and a new state, Haryana.

In the 1967 state assembly elections the Akalis had won a quarter of the vote in the Punjab and had formed a coalition government with Jana Sangh, the Communists, and Congress dissidents. They had re- mained in power until 1971 when the government fell and president's rule was established. In the 1972 state assembly elections, the Congress party had won a majority of seats. The Akali Dal was opposed to the emergency and to the Congress party and in the 1977 parliamentary elections allied itself with the Janata party.

The National Conference is a Muslim party and the leading

party in Jammu and Kashmir. Led by Sheikh Abdullah, it was antagonistic to the Congress party until 1975, when Sheikh Abdullah returned to power as chief minister of the state with the support of the Congress majority. While elsewhere in India many Muslim organizations ended their traditional ties with the government to endorse the Janata party in 1977, in Kashmir the National Conference formed an electoral alliance with Congress.[7]

In the 1977 parliamentary elections, therefore, the regional and national opposition parties generally allied themselves with one or the other of the two main protagonists, Congress and Janata. Congress put up 493 candidates for the 542 parliamentary seats and had an electoral alliance with the Communist party of India (which put up 91 candidates), the National Conference in Jammu and Kashmir, the AIADMK in Tamil Nadu, and several small local parties. The Janata party and the Congress for Democracy put up 423 candidates and formed electoral alliances with the CPM (which put up 53 candidates), the DMK in Tamil Nadu, and the Akali Dal in the Punjab. In no previous election in postindependence India had the party lines been so sharply drawn between two major political groups.

---

[7] For a detailed account of the role of Muslim parties in the 1977 parliamentary elections and an analysis of Muslim voting patterns, see Theodore P. Wright, Jr., "Muslims and the 1977 Indian Elections: A Watershed?" *Asian Survey*, vol. 17, no. 12 (December 1977), pp. 1207–1220.

5

New Delhi: The Returns Come In

New Delhi was tense on March 19, just a day before the counting was to begin.[1] Rumors spread around the city that the government might provoke violence at the counting stations and then exploit it as a pretext for calling in the border security forces or the army to "restore order." Only a few days before, Mrs. Gandhi had accused the opposition of fomenting violence and hatred and the press of adopting antinational positions—charges that were strikingly similar to those she had made when declaring the emergency twenty months before. In reply, Lal K. Advani, general secretary of the Janata party, had issued a statement quoting the election commissioner who had commended all of the political parties for their exemplary conduct during the campaign. Janata leaders made a special point of urging their followers to exercise restraint and to avoid any provocative demonstrations, especially at the counting stations. When the report came in that an attempt had been made on Sanjay Gandhi's life while he was traveling in his jeep in Amethi constituency, they greeted it with derision.

It was rumored that Mrs. Gandhi had asked the military to go on the alert during the counting of the ballots but that the military had advised that this was not necessary. The night of the nineteenth, word spread around the city that an unusually large number of police

---

[1] Balloting was spread over four days from March 16 through March 20, with a day's break on March 17. Counting began on the morning of March 20, but returning officers did not announce any returns until the evening after all constituencies had voted. A large part of India's administrative machinery was assigned to manage the four days of polling: 1,540,000 officers were assigned to man 383,000 polling stations for an electorate of 320 million, 46 million more than in the 1971 parliamentary elections. On an average, there was a polling station for every 900 people. Polling stations were open from 8 a.m. to 4 p.m. but those in line at closing time were permitted to vote. Approximately a million ballot boxes were required.

had been seen moving toward one of the counting stations in the southern part of New Delhi. Several journalists from the *Indian Express* rushed to the counting station only to find a number of young Janata poll watchers unpacking their bedrolls from their motorcycles; they planned to spend the long night watching over the sealed ballot boxes until the counting began the next morning.

By March 20 the government-run Press Information Bureau and several of the newspapers had placed large billboards around the city, where the returns would be posted by state as they came in. Though no returns were expected until after five o'clock in the evening, crowds of people began to assemble around the billboards early in the afternoon.

The Election Commission's policy was to announce the results in any parliamentary constituency only when all the ballots in that constituency had been counted. However, since each of the candidates had his own poll watchers inside the counting stations, word of who was leading leaked out during the day. Party workers and journalists began receiving initial returns in the early evening. Though none of these were posted or broadcast, word spread to the crowds that Janata was sweeping northern India. The earliest returns posted on the billboards and announced on the radio, however, were from the south where Congress was winning, and throughout the night All India Radio (popularly known as All Indira Radio) held back reports of Janata victories. But even as the billboards reported Congress leads, the crowds cheered Janata victories. Their enthusiasm reached a climax when the returns came in from Delhi and New Delhi, where Janata had taken all seven seats, all by overwhelming margins.

The first report of Indira Gandhi's defeat came before midnight on the BBC, whose Hindi service had a huge audience. On the twenty-first, the morning newspapers confirmed the news. Mrs. Gandhi had polled 122,000 votes, Raj Narain 177,000. It was a particularly sweet victory for Narain, a socialist member of the Janata party and a special enemy of Indira Gandhi's. She had defeated Narain by a huge margin in the 1971 parliamentary elections, and later Narain had accused her of violating the election law. This was the charge that had eventually prompted the Allahabad High Court to rule that Mrs. Gandhi should step down as a member of Parliament and thus had precipitated the declaration of a national emergency. Raj Narain had been among the first arrested.

In the nearby constituency of Amethi, Sanjay Gandhi was defeated. His opponent won 176,000 votes against Sanjay's 100,000 in a constituency that had previously overwhelmingly elected a Con-

Waiting for the election returns on Parliament Street in New Delhi.

gress candidate. Sanjay's ally Bansi Lal was defeated too, as were Vidhya Charan Shukla, the minister of information and broadcasting, and Haribhau Ramchandra Gokhale, minister of law and justice. In the morning edition of the *Indian Express*, the popular cartoonist Abu made his comment on the defeat of the information minister. The cartoon showed two men listening to All India Radio, with the caption: "V.C. Shukla has lost? Is the news reliable?"

Virtually all of the leaders of the Janata party and the Congress for Democracy were elected, often by staggeringly large margins. George Fernandes, the Socialist trade unionist, won his seat with a margin of 330,000 votes, although (some say because) he was in jail during the entire election campaign and was unable to visit his constituency.

In the streets of Delhi, taxi and motor rickshaw drivers slowed down at each of the billboards to see the latest word on who had been elected or defeated. One rickshaw driver laughed when he saw the flash announcement on the billboard in front of the *Hindustan Times* which said "Sanjay quits politics." Asked why he laughed, the driver replied in English, "We threw Sanjay out and now he

59

says he is quitting!" People seemed elated by the knowledge of what their votes had done. At the large billboard on Parliament Street a group was asked who they thought would be India's next prime minister. Did they prefer Morarji Desai, Jagjivan Ram, or Charan Singh? "It doesn't matter," said one of the men. "If we don't like the prime minister we can always replace him."

All day long various political leaders issued statements explaining why the voters had turned the Congress party out. Atal Behari Vajpayee, the Janata party leader (and a few days later India's minister for external affairs), said that the election had been "more like a referendum than an ordinary election." The people had voted against "coercion, regimentation, and intimidation. . . . They voted for freedom, cooperation, and for an open system and society." The Imam of Jama Masjid attributed the victory of the Janata party to the unity of Hindus and Muslims, and said, "It is not the Congress that has been defeated but oppression." When newsmen asked Morarji Desai whether he considered this his finest hour, he graciously replied, "This is the country's finest hour. Everything that Gandhiji stood for has been vindicated."[2]

Raj Narain attributed his own remarkable victory against Indira Gandhi to the arrest of leaders like Jayaprakash Narayan and Morarji Desai and to the government's mistaken notion that family planning and forced sterilization were the same thing. A. Palkhiwala, a noted constitutional lawyer who had spoken out frequently against the amendments to the Constitution, declared: "History will record that the true gains of the emergency have been the unification of the opposition, the sharp awakening of the political conscience of the nation, and the dawn of realization among the people that they are the only keepers of the Constitution." And Jayaprakash Narayan pronounced: "The people have made their choice. They have opted for liberty. I trust they will not ever relent their vigil."

Tendering her resignation, Indira Gandhi said, "The collective judgment of the people must be respected. My colleagues and I accept their verdict unreservedly and in a spirit of humility." Sanjay announced that he was quitting active politics and added, "I am all the more sorry if what I did in my personal capacity has recoiled on my mother whose life has been spent in selfless service." The president of the Congress party in Delhi blamed "demolitions, unimaginative enforcement of the pricetagging order, and up to a small extent the family planning drive" for the defeat of the Congress party in

---

[2] The quotations in this paragraph and the next are from *Times of India*, March 22, 1977.

Delhi.[3] But the *National Herald*, the Allahabad and Delhi newspaper closely tied to the Nehru family and to Mrs. Gandhi, attributed the defeat of the Congress party to "vilification and misrepresentation."[4] In a remarkable turnaround, most of the other newspapers that had supported Indira Gandhi now heralded the victory of the Janata party as a victory for democracy. In a long article, the editor of the *Times of India*, who had cautiously supported Mrs. Gandhi during the emergency, denounced the destruction of democracy and human rights during the emergency and welcomed the return to democratic government.

But another point of view, a minority one perhaps, deserves to be recorded. A senior government official who had spent his career in relatively nonpolitical ministries expressed thus his alarm at Mrs. Gandhi's defeat:

> Sometimes I think we are a suicidal pople. Whenever we are close to doing something successful, we pull back. There are rare moments in our history when we came close to having a leadership capable of pulling the country together. There was Ashoka and Chandragupta and Akbar and Curzon. They each had their own ways of doing things. So did Mrs. Gandhi. Now that she is overthrown, just when we had a chance of uniting the country, we will be replacing her with satraps, regional leaders who will pull in different directions without a central national leader. The south is not with this government and each of these Janata leaders will start to build their own centers of power in the states. These people talk about decentralizing power but that's only another way of talking about giving power to themselves.[5]

In the first days after the elections speculation centered on the new government. The leadership of the Janata party and the Congress for Democracy were expected to meet on the twenty-fourth to choose India's new prime minister; the members of Parliament from both groups would gather at Rajghat, the memorial to Mahatma Gandhi, to take an oath of service to the country, and later in the day Jayaprakash was expected to meet with Morarji Desai and Jagjivan Ram. Representatives of the third contender, Charan Singh, who was ill, were also expected to take part in the discussion. It was generally expected that Morarji would be chosen, since he was the senior leader of the Janata party and deserved the position because of his consistent opposition to Indira Gandhi over nearly a decade.

---

[3] These quotations are from the *Statesman*, March 23, 1977.
[4] *National Herald*, March 23, 1977.
[5] Interview with the author.

Morarji Desai was in his eighties, Charan Singh was in his seventies, and Jagjivan Ram was sixty-eight. All three were former Congressmen, all were experienced government officials, and all were reassuring figures to the bureaucracy, the business community, and the country as a whole. There was a sense, moreover, that these three men represented the last of the nationalist generation. Those in the next tier of leadership in the Janata party were all in their forties or fifties. Among those who had emerged as national figures during the emergency and the elections were: George Fernandes, the trade union leader who escaped into the underground until his arrest a few months before the elections on charges of fomenting an armed attack; Subramanian Swami, the Harvard-M.I.T.–trained economist who sneaked in and out of India during the emergency under the eyes of a police establishment that reportedly had been infiltrated by his fellow Jana Sangh members; Chandra Shekhar, perhaps the most popular and charismatic figure of the socialist Young Turks, a member of the Congress party until he and some of his supporters were arrested and, according to some, a potential prime minister; Mohan Dharia, another Young Turk in the Congress party who had resigned from Mrs. Gandhi's cabinet shortly before the emergency and who, like Chandra Shekhar, is widely regarded as a man of great principle; Atal Behari Vajpayee, respected as a spokesman for the new more secular nationalist Jana Sangh; and Lal K. Advani, another young Jana Sangh leader who served as secretary of the Janata party, carefully minding the central office while the national leaders were on the campaign trail.

Many observers feared that if Jagjivan Ram's Congress for Democracy did not merge with the Janata party there might be conflict between the two parties soon, especially if the Congress party began to fall apart. Although the election seemed to have produced a two-party system (or, more accurately, a two-and-a-half party system), the fragility of the Congress party and the independent status of the Congress for Democracy made the party structure unstable. Chandra Shekhar, describing the party system as very fluid, predicted: "the situation in the states and in the central government may look very different a year from now."[6]

On March 23, even before a new government had been chosen, the government revoked the proclamation of emergency issued on June 26, 1975, and lifted the ban on twenty-six organizations including the RSS and Jammaat-e-Islami. The central government advised the state governments to release all political détenus. The government

---

[6] Interview with the author.

also issued an order ending press censorship and withdrew the circulars asking government departments, public sector enterprises, and other government bodies not to advertise in the *Statesman* and the *Indian Express*. The Janata party secretary announced that among the first acts of the new government would be the repeal of the Prevention of Publication of Objectionable Matters Act, a review of the Maintenance of Internal Security Act, and the rescinding of the Forty-Second Amendment to the Constitution.

Abu's cartoon for the day portrayed an elderly villager squatting on the ground smoking his hookah. The old man was asking Jayaprakash Narayan, "Has my revolution been as total as you wished it to be?"[7]

---

[7] *Indian Express*, March 23, 1977.

PART TWO
Analysis of the Results

6

The Election Returns

Nationally the Janata party and the Congress for Democracy won 298 seats; together, they and their allies took a total of 328 seats out of 542. Congress won 153 seats. The Janata party alone won 271, or just half of the seats in Parliament (see Tables 2 and 3).[1]

The magnitude of the Congress defeat, especially in northern India, came as a surprise even to the Janata leaders, who had expected their party to win. In many constituencies, Janata's margin of victory was enormous. In Uttar Pradesh and Bihar, many Congress candidates who had won with 40 percent or more of the vote in the 1971 elections dropped to 20 and even 15 percent. It was clear that the Janata victory reflected not simply the consolidation of the opposition vote, but a substantial shift away from the Congress party. In almost every state the rise in the Janata party vote over what the constituent parties had won in 1971 was substantially greater than the decline in the Congress vote. The Congress losses in constituencies

---

[1] Since victory is by a plurality in single-member constituencies, the party with the largest popular vote tends to have a disproportionately large share of parliamentary seats. In four of the five previous parliamentary elections Congress, with a popular vote between 43.6 and 47.8 percent, won more than two-thirds of the seats. In the 1977 elections, the Janata party won 55 percent of the seats with 43.2 percent of the popular vote. There have been various attempts to calculate what Eric da Costa of the Indian Institute of Public Opinion has called the Multiplier—the relation of seats won to votes cast. For a review, see Norman D. Palmer, *Elections and Political Development: The South Asian Experience* (Durham: Duke University Press, 1975), pp. 40–42. For a useful preelection compendium of materials on the 1977 elections, see *Briefing Materials on the Indian Parliamentary Elections, 1977*, prepared by Philip Oldenburg and edited by Marshall M. Bouton for the Indian Council of the Asia Society and the Center for South Asian Studies of Columbia University, March 1977. Election figures for the 1971 parliamentary elections have been taken from *Report of the Fifth General Election to the House of the People of India, 1971*, vol. 2 (statistical), Election Commission of India, New Delhi, 1973. 1977 figures are based on materials made available by the Election Commission.

TABLE 2

Election Data, Indian Parliamentary Elections, 1952–1977

Year	Seats	Candi-dates	Elec-torate (in millions)	Polling Stations	Votes Polled (in millions)	Turnout
1952	489	1,864	173.2	132,600	80.7	45.7
1957	494	1,519	193.7	220,500	91.3	47.8
1962	494	1,985	217.7	238,400	119.9	55.4
1967	520	2,369	250.1	267,500	152.7	61.3
1971	518	2,784	274.1	342,900	151.5	55.3
1977	542	2,439	318.3	373,700	193.7	60.4

SOURCE: *General Election 1977, Reference Hand Book.*

TABLE 3

Parliamentary Election Results, 1971 and 1977

Party	1971 Seats won	1971 Percentage of valid votes		1977 Seats won	1977 Percentage of valid votes
Congress	352	43.6		153	34.5
Janata				298	43.2
Congress O.	16	10.4			
Jana Sangh	22	7.4			
Swatantra[a]	8	3.1	53 27.6		
Socialists	5	3.5			
Bharatiya Lok Dal[b]	2	3.2			
CPI	23	4.9		7	2.8
CPM	25	5.1		21	4.3
DMK	23	3.8		1 ⎱	4.7
AIADMK				18 ⎰	
Akali Dal				8 ⎱	
Independents	14	8.3		14 ⎰	10.5
Others				19 ⎰	
Total	518	100.0		539	100.0

[a] Merged with the Bharatiya Lok Dal in 1974.
[b] Includes the Bharatiya Kranti Dal, the Utkal Congress, and the Bangla Congress, although they actually united (along with a few smaller parties) to form the Bharatiya Lok Dal after the 1971 elections.
SOURCE: *Report of the Fifth General Election to the House of the People of India,* 1971, vol. 2 (statistical), Election Commission of India, New Delhi, 1973. 1977 figures based on materials made available by the Election Commission and by the Ministry of Broadcasting and Information, New Delhi.

reserved for Harijan candidates and in constituencies with substantial Muslim votes were at least as large as, and in many instances even larger than, those in other constituencies. One of the largest margins of victory for a Janata candidate came in the Delhi constituency that contained the slum dwellers resettled as part of Sanjay Gandhi's beautification program. Indira Gandhi, her rhetoric notwithstanding, had failed to win over India's poorest classes.

We turn now to an analysis of some of the variations in the election results. Although the absence of systematic polling data is a handicap, by studying regional and social patterns and the behavior of selected constituencies we can gain a more complete view of how different groups responded to the campaign and to the emergency itself.

Regional Variations

The most striking feature of the results was the regional schism they revealed: 221 of the 298 seats won by Janata and the Congress for Democracy were in the predominantly Hindi-speaking region in the north of India that had been the historic base of the Congress party's power. In a dramatic reversal, Congress won only 2 seats in the north. The two western states, Maharashtra and Gujarat, were more evenly split, with 35 seats for the Janata party and 32 for Congress. In the northeast (West Bengal, Orissa, Assam, and the hill states) 35 seats went to Janata, 23 to Congress, and 17 to the Communist party Marxist which had supported Janata. But the pattern was markedly different in south India. Altogether in the four southern states, the Congress party won 92 out of 129 seats, as against only 6 for Janata. In other words, 75 percent of all the seats won by the Janata party and the Congress for Democracy were from seven northern Hindi-speaking states and the capital city, while 60 percent of the seats won by the Congress party were from the four states of south India, where Congress was able to maintain its traditional strength. It was evident that the worst manifestations of the emergency had not reached south of the Vindhyas.

Regional issues were decisive in at least two of the southern states. In Tamil Nadu, as we have seen, the contest was largely between the two regional parties, the DMK which had governed the state until the middle of 1976 and which was widely accused of corruption, and the reformist All India Anna DMK. The latter party won the largest number of seats in the state, eighteen out of thirty-nine (see Table 3).

In Kerala, the Congress victory was part of a larger sweep for

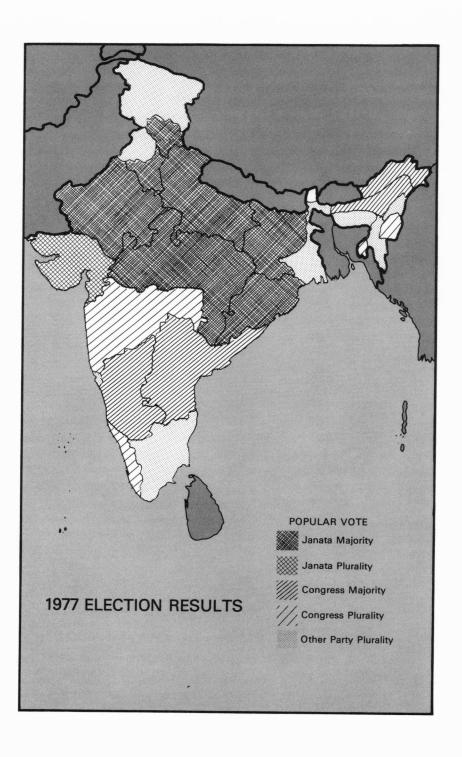

POPULAR VOTE

Janata Majority

Janata Plurality

Congress Majority

Congress Plurality

Other Party Plurality

1977 ELECTION RESULTS

TABLE 4

State	Total Seats	Congress	Janata	CPI	CPM	Other Parties	Independent
Andhra Pradesh	42	41	1				
Assam	14	10	3				1
Bihar	54		52				2
Gujarat	26	10	16				
Haryana	10		10				
Himachal Pradesh	4		3				
Jammu and Kashmir	6	2				2	1
Karnataka	28	26	2				
Kerala	20	11		4		5	
Madhya Pradesh	40	1	37			1	1
Maharashtra	48	20	19		3	5	1
Manipur	2	2					
Meghalaya	2	1				1	
Nagaland	1					1	
Orissa	21	4	15		1		1
Punjab	13		3		1	8	
Rajasthan	25	1	24				
Sikkim	1	1					
Tamil Nadu	39	14	3	3		19	
Tripura	2	1	1				
Uttar Pradesh	85		85				
West Bengal	42	3	16		16	2	5
Andaman and Nicobar Islands	1	1					
Arunachal Pradesh	2	1					1
Chandigarh	1		1				
Dadra and Nagar Haveli	1	1					
Delhi	7		7				
Goa, Daman, and Diu	2	1				1	
Lakshadweep	1	1					
Mizoram	1						1
Pondicherry	1					1	
Total[a]	542	153	298	7	21	46	14

[a] Elections were postponed in three constituencies (one each in Himachal, Jammu and Kashmir, and Punjab). Thus the seats won by the parties add to 539 rather than 542.
SOURCE: See Table 3.

TABLE 5

DISTRIBUTION OF SEATS, BY STATE, PARLIAMENTARY ELECTION OF 1971

State	Total Seats	Congress	"Janata"[a]	CPI	CPM	Others
Andhra Pradesh	41	28		1	1	11[b]
Assam	14	13				1
Bihar	53	39	7	5		2
Gujarat	24	11	13			
Haryana	9	7	1			1
Himachal Pradesh	4	4				
Jammu and Kashmir	6	5				1
Karnataka	27	27				
Kerala	19	6		3	2	8
Madhya Pradesh	37	21	12			4
Maharashtra	45	42	1			2
Orissa	20	15	4	1		
Punjab	13	10		2		1
Rajasthan	23	14	7			2
Tamil Nadu	39	9	1	4		25[c]
Uttar Pradesh	85	73	6	4		2
West Bengal	40	13	2	3	20	2
Delhi	7	7				
Other States and Union Territories[d]	12	8			2	2
Total	518	352	54	23	25	65

[a] Includes Congress O., Jana Sangh, the Samyukta Socialist party, Bharatiya Kranti Dal, the Praja Socialist party, the Utkal Congress, the Swatantra party, and the Bangla Congress.

[b] The Telangana Praja Samiti (a regional party in the western districts of Andhra which merged with Congress in 1975) won ten of these seats.

[c] The DMK, which had an electoral alliance with Congress, won twenty-three of these seats.

[d] Andaman and Nicobar, Chandigarh, Dadra and Nagar Haveli, Goa, Lakshadweep, Manipur, Nagaland, Pondicherry, and Tripura.

SOURCE: See Table 3.

a united front coalition which included the Congress, the pro-Soviet Communist party of India, and the Muslim League, a coalition which had successfully governed the state for six years (see Table 4). Kerala was the only state that held state assembly elections at the same time as the parliamentary elections, and these too were swept by the united front.

That the south was not wholly unaffected by the emergency is revealed by the outcome in terms of votes polled rather than seats won in the two states closest to northern India, Andhra and Karnataka. In Andhra, Congress had won 55.8 percent of the vote in the

1971 elections but had lost virtually all of the constituencies in the western part of the state (and 14.4 percent of the state-wide vote) to the Telangana Praja Samiti (TPS), a local party that had called for the secession of the western part of the state and the formation of a new Telangana state. In 1975 after politicians from the western region were incorporated into the state government, the Telangana Praja Samiti had merged with Congress. In all, then, the Congress party might have expected to win as much as 70 percent of the vote in Andhra. In fact, it won 57.4 percent, a whopping majority but less than the vote Congress and the TPS had won in 1971. The Janata party vote increased from the 12 percent won by the relevant opposition parties in 1971 to 32 percent in 1977. The decline of Congress was even clearer in the neighboring state of Karnataka. There Congress had won 71 percent of the vote in 1971 and declined to 57 percent in 1977, while Janata's share increased from 24 percent to 40 percent (see Tables 6 and 7). Still, the Janata party won only a handful of seats in all of south India. High on the political agenda of the new government would be measures to attract southern support.

In a few states in the north the Janata victory seemed more the result of the consolidation of the opposition than of any decline in support for Congress. In Orissa, Congress more or less held its own with about 38 percent of the vote in both 1971 and 1977, and the Janata-CFD vote in 1977 was only slightly higher than the constituent Janata groups had won in 1971. One explanation, perhaps, is that the leader of the CFD, Nandini Satpathy, had herself been the Congress chief minister of the state until a few months before the election, making it difficult for the opposition to effectively accuse others of responsibility for the emergency measures.

More surprising was the vote in Gujarat, the state whose opposition to Indira Gandhi and the local Congress government had been most militant in 1974 and 1975 and where the Janata Front, precurser of the national Janata party, had been formed. Janata won sixteen seats compared with ten for Congress, but both parties remained close to their 1971 vote, with a slight improvement for Congress and a corresponding drop for Janata. Ironically, this state may have been spared some of the excesses because a Janata government was actually in power during the first nine months of the emergency. Congress improved slightly in West Bengal, but its ally, the CPI, dropped precipitously. The Janata vote jumped from 12.9 percent to 21.5 percent.

Elsewhere the Congress decline was massive. In Haryana, Himachal, Jammu and Kashmir, and Delhi, Congress declined by more than thirty percentage points over its showing in the 1971 parliamentary

TABLE 6

CONGRESS PARTY VOTE, BY STATE, 1971 AND 1977
(vote in percentages, differences in percentage points)

State	1971	1977	Difference
Andhra Pradesh	55.8[a]	57.4	+ 1.6
Assam	57.0	50.6	− 6.4
Bihar	40.1	22.9	−17.2
Gujarat	45.3	46.9	+ 1.6
Haryana	52.6	18.0	−34.6
Himachal Pradesh	77.0	38.3	−38.7
Jammu and Kashmir	53.9	15.2	−38.7
Karnataka	70.8	56.8	−14.0
Kerala	19.8	29.1	+ 9.3
Madhya Pradesh	45.5	32.5	−13.0
Maharashtra	63.5	47.0	−16.5
Manipur	30.1	45.3	+15.2
Nagaland	39.5	46.6	+ 7.1
Orissa	38.4	38.2	− 0.2
Punjab	45.9	35.9	−10.0
Rajasthan	50.3	30.6	−19.7
Tamil Nadu	12.5	22.3	+ 9.8
Tripura	36.3	39.7	+ 3.4
Uttar Pradesh	48.0	25.0	−23.0
West Bengal	27.7	31.7	+ 4.0
Delhi	64.5	30.2	−34.3
Total, India	43.6	34.5	− 9.1

[a] In the 1971 elections Congress was opposed by the Telangana Praja Samiti (TPS) which subsequently merged with Congress. This figure does not include the 14.4 percent won by the TPS in 1971.
SOURCE: See Table 3.

elections. And in the states of Bihar, Punjab, Maharashtra, Madhya Pradesh, Rajasthan, and Uttar Pradesh, Congress dropped between ten and twenty-three percentage points (see Table 6). The magnitude of these defeats left the Congress governments in these states in a precarious position, without popular support and threatened by defections from within.

Urban/Rural Voting Patterns

While the extent of the north-south division was unexpected, even more unexpected to some observers (including, one suspects, Indira Gandhi) was the absence of a division between rural and urban India. In those parts of the country where the Janata party won, it

TABLE 7

"JANATA PARTY" VOTE, BY STATE, 1971 AND 1977
(vote in percentages, differences in percentage points)

State	1971[a]	1977[b]	Difference
Andhra Pradesh	12.1	32.3	+20.2
Assam	11.6	35.8	+24.2
Bihar	34.0	65.0	+31.0
Gujarat	48.6	49.5	+ 0.9
Haryana	25.6	70.4	+44.8
Himachal Pradesh	17.7	58.4	+40.7
Jammu and Kashmir	13.1	13.8	+ 0.7
Karnataka	24.2	39.9	+15.7
Kerala	6.1	7.2	+ 1.1
Madhya Pradesh	38.7	58.0	+19.3
Maharashtra	12.5	33.2	+20.7
Manipur	14.2	8.6	− 5.6
Nagaland[c]	—	—	—
Orissa	50.6	51.8	+ 1.2
Punjab	9.9	13.0	+ 3.1
Rajasthan	31.3	65.2	+33.9
Tamil Nadu	40.7	16.1	−24.6
Tripura	0.5	17.8	+17.3
Uttar Pradesh	38.0	68.0	+30.0
West Bengal	12.9	21.5	+ 8.6
Delhi	31.4	68.2	+36.8
Total, India	27.7	43.2	+15.5

[a] Combined vote for Congress O., Jana Sangh, the Samyukta Socialist party, Bharatiya Kranti Dal, the Praja Socialist party, the Utkal Congress, the Swatantra party, and the Bangla Congress.
[b] Combined vote for Janata party, Congress for Democracy, and in Tamil Nadu the Congress O.
[c] Janata contested no constituencies in Nagaland.
SOURCE: See Table 3.

did equally well in urban and rural constituencies. All seven seats in Delhi, for example, went to Janata candidates, but so did all the surrounding rural constituencies in the Punjab, Haryana, and nearby Uttar Pradesh. Janata also won the urban constituencies of Varanasi, Lucknow, Allahabad, Agra, Meerut, and Kanpur, all in Uttar Pradesh, where Janata swept all of the eighty-five seats. Similarly, the Janata party and its allies won all of the urban seats in and around Calcutta and all but three seats in the state of West Bengal. (For the results in India's largest cities see Table 8.)

In all Congress won only one seat (in Madras) out of the twenty-one seats in the four metropolitan cities of Delhi, Bombay, Calcutta, and Madras, as against fifteen in 1971. But in most of the country the elections demonstrated that urban and rural areas in India tended to be affected by much the same influences and voted in much the same way.

In south India the Congress party and its allies did nearly as

TABLE 8

DISTRIBUTION OF SEATS IN INDIA'S LARGEST CITIES, 1967–1971–1977

Party	Calcutta 67–71–77	Bombay 67–71–77	Madras 67–71–77	Delhi 67–71–77
Congress	2–2–0	4–6–0	0–0–1	1–7–0
"Janata party"	0–0–3	1–0–4	0–0–1	6–0–7
CPI	1–1–0	1–0–0	0–0–0	0–0–0
CPM	2–2–2	0–0–1	0–0–0	0–0–0
Other parties	0–0–0	0–0–1	2–2–1	0–0–0
Independents	0–0–0	0–0–0	0–0–0	0–0–0

Party	Hyderabad 67–71–77	Ahmadabad 67–71–77	Bangalore 67–71–77	Kanpur 67–71–77
Congress	2–0–2	1–1–1	2–2–1	0–0–0
"Janata party"	0–0–0	0–1–0	0–0–1	0–0–1
CPI	0–0–0	0–0–0	0–0–0	0–0–0
CPM	0–0–0	0–0–0	0–0–0	0–0–0
Other parties	0–2–0	0–0–0	0–0–0	0–0–0
Independents	0–0–0	1–0–1	0–0–0	1–1–0

Party	Poona 67–71–77	Nagpur 67–71–77	Lucknow 67–71–77	Coimbatore 67–71–77
Congress	0–1–0	1–0–1	0–1–0	0–0–0
"Janata party"	1–0–1	0–0–0	0–0–1	0–0–0
CPI	0–0–0	0–0–0	0–0–0	1–1–1
CPM	0–0–0	0–0–0	0–0–0	0–0–0
Other parties	0–0–0	0–1–0	0–0–0	0–0–0
Independents	0–0–0	0–0–0	1–0–0	0–0–0

Party	Madurai 67–71–77	Jaipur 67–71–77	Agra 67–71–77	Varanasi 67–71–77
Congress	0–1–1	0–0–0	1–1–0	0–1–0
"Janata party"	0–0–0	1–1–1	0–0–1	0–0–1
CPI	1–0–0	0–0–0	0–0–0	1–0–0
CPM	0–0–0	0–0–0	0–0–0	0–0–0
Other parties	0–0–0	0–0–0	0–0–0	0–0–0
Independents	0–0–0	0–0–0	0–0–0	0–0–0

TABLE 8 (continued)

Party	Indore 67–71–77	Jabalpur 67–71–77	Allahabad 67–71–77
Congress	1–1–0	1–1–0	1–1–0
"Janata party"	0–0–1	0–0–1	0–0–1
CPI	0–0–0	0–0–0	0–0–0
CPM	0–0–0	0–0–0	0–0–0
Other parties	0–0–0	0–0–0	0–0–0
Independents	0–0–0	0–0–0	0–0–0

Summary, all Nineteen Cities:

Party	67–71–77
Congress	17–26–7
"Janata party"	9–2–25
CPI	5–2–1
CPM	2–2–3
Other parties	2–5–2
Independents	3–1–1
Total	38–38–39

NOTE: Included are cities with populations exceeding half a million at the 1971 census.
SOURCE: See Table 3; also *Report of the Fourth General Election to the House of the People*, 1967, vol. 2 (statistical), Election Commission of India, New Delhi, 1969.

well in the urban constituencies as they did in the rural areas. In Tamil Nadu, for example, Congress and its allies won two of the three seats in the city of Madras and carried the urban constituencies of industrial Coimbatore and Madurai. In Andhra, where Congress won forty-one out of the forty-two seats, Congress carried both of the urban seats in the city of Hyderabad. Congress, though with a reduced margin of votes, swept the state of Karnataka, losing only one of the two urban seats in the city of Bangalore. Only in the state of Maharashtra in western India was there a substantial difference between the voting behavior of urban and rural constituencies. The Janata party and its allies swept all six seats in Bombay and carried Poona but won only half of the constituencies in the state as a whole. Congress carried the urban constituencies in Nagpur and Sholapur. Surprisingly, Congress also carried both Ahmadabad (by a small margin) and Baroda, the two largest urban centers in Gujarat, a state where the party won only ten of the twenty-six seats.

In the Punjab, Congress lost both urban seats, Amritsar and Ludhiana, but the margins were smaller than in the rural areas of the state. Similarly, in Madhya Pradesh the anti-Congress vote was higher in the countryside than in three of the state's four urban constituencies. The anti-Congress wave also swept every urban center in Uttar Pradesh, but the rural vote against Congress exceeded the anti-Congress vote in four of the state's six predominantly urban constituencies. In West Bengal, too, Congress did better in urban than in rural constituencies.

On the other hand in Bihar, where Congress won only 23 percent of the vote, the party did even worse than its state average in two of the three cities and won as little as 8.2 percent of the vote in Patna which had been a major center of anti-Congress agitation prior to the emergency. And as we have noted, in Karnataka and Andhra the anti-Congress vote was generally higher in the urban centers.

In all there were forty-seven urban constituencies (that is, with more than 350,000 urban dwellers) contested by the Congress party in thirteen states; in twenty-three of these the Congress vote exceeded the state-wide average, while in the remaining twenty-four it fell below the state-wide average. In thirty-two urban constituencies Janata did better than in the surrounding rural areas, while in only seven urban constituencies did it do worse (see Table 9).

In short, the urban areas were not always more antigovernment than the rural areas, but the Janata party proved to be more effective at consolidating the opposition vote in urban than in rural constituencies. Fewer independents and fewer candidates from the smaller parties fragmented the opposition vote in the urban constituencies. Urban areas in the 1977 elections proved to be no more anti- or progovernment than the rest of India, neither more radical nor more conservative, but they did prove to be more electorally polarized in the sense that the two-party vote was generally higher in urban than in rural constituencies.

Urban/Rural Patterns in the Recent Past. There is evidence from earlier elections that India's urban constituencies tend to resemble—both in voter turnout and in party preferences—the rural areas in which they are located more closely than they resemble each other. This pattern evidently persisted in 1977. In a recent study of *state assembly* elections it was found that voter turnout was generally higher in urban than in rural areas in the 1957 and 1962 elections, but that the gap narrowed in 1967 and 1972, when rural turnout increased.[2] A larger share of the urban vote also went to protest

---

[2] Myron Weiner and John Osgood Field, "India's Urban Constituencies," *Comparative Politics*, vol. 8, no. 2 (January 1976), pp. 183–222.

TABLE 9

COMPARISON BETWEEN THE CONGRESS VOTE IN URBAN CONSTITUENCIES
AND IN THE SURROUNDING STATES, 1977
(in percentages and percentage points)

State (number of urban constituencies in parentheses)	Congress Vote		
	Average for urban constituencies	State-wide	Difference
Andhra Pradesh (3)	48.5	57.4	−8.9
Bihar (3)	18.4	22.9	−4.5
Gujarat (4)	48.4	46.9	+1.5
Karnataka (5)	53.9	56.8	−2.9
Madhya Pradesh (4)	32.4	32.5	−0.1
Maharashtra (10)	40.0	47.0	−7.0
Uttar Pradesh (6)	25.8	25.0	+0.8
West Bengal (6)	36.5	31.7	+4.8
India (55)	37.6	34.5 (national)	+3.1

NOTE: Only states where Congress contested at least three urban constituencies
are included.
SOURCE: See Table 3.

parties of the left or right, particularly to the Communists and Jana
Sangh. This was especially true in the 1967 elections for both state
and national parliaments: Congress was routed in much of urban
India even while it held a majority of the rural constituencies (albeit
with a declining share of the vote).

When Congress lost many of the state assembly elections to the
opposition parties in the 1967 elections and barely won a majority in
Parliament, many Congress leaders concluded that the major threat
had come from the parties on the right, especially Jana Sangh whose
electoral following had grown considerably throughout northern
India. But Indira Gandhi had argued that the important factor was
a simple antiestablishment vote and that a more radical program
would attract support from the lower-income groups in the countryside as well as from the working and middle class in the urban
centers. Her break with the conservatives within the Congress followed soon afterwards, leading to the formation of the Congress O.
under Morarji Desai. Most of the policies adopted by Mrs. Gandhi
after 1967, and especially after the 1969 split, seem to have been
geared toward winning the approval of urban voters: the nationaliza-
tion of banks, a ceiling on urban property, and attacks on the princes

and industrialists. By the time of the 1971 parliamentary elections it was evident that Mrs. Gandhi had captured the protest sentiment of urban Indians. Lower-echelon civil servants, taxi drivers, university professors, and students became her most enthusiastic supporters. Some of the largest demonstrations on her behalf were in New Delhi, hitherto a center of Jana Sangh strength.

Mrs. Gandhi's strategy of radicalizing the party to halt the drift of voters to right-wing parties proved effective. The ruling Congress party swept the polls in the parliamentary elections in 1971, especially in the urban areas; Congress won thirty-three of the fifty-two predominantly urban parliamentary constituencies (as against eighteen in 1967) and captured all nine of the urban parliamentary constituencies previously won by Jana Sangh. The trend continued in the 1972 state assembly elections when Congress won four of every five urban seats.

After 1972 Congress again began to lose urban support. Severe inflation in 1974 and 1975 (estimated at 30 percent) was accompanied, to quote from a resolution of the Congress Working Committee, by "organized strikes, go slow movements by government employees, railway employees and industrial employees . . . acts of sabotage paralyzing the railway and communication systems . . . student agitations and indiscipline"—all of them urban centered.[3] Moreover, the urban press, both in English and in the regional languages, was becoming more critical of the Congress governments. This was the period when the major urban protest movements got underway in Gujarat (eventually leading to the formation of the Janata Front), then in Bihar, and when the police mutinied in Uttar Pradesh. By 1974 the government was evidently paying the political price for high inflation and for a development strategy that had placed too little stress on increasing employment to meet the growth of the labor force; its educational strategy, at the same time, had resulted in a rapid increase in the urban middle class. Pressed by unemployment and inflation, the urban middle class had turned to a variety of protest movements in the 1960s and early 1970s, including sons of the soil nativist movements in Bombay, Bangalore, Gauhati, and Hyderabad; the Jana Sangh with its nationalist appeal; the revolutionary Naxalites, who attracted many urban educated youth; and a variety of student and youth movements. The same forces had precipitated factional struggles for power within Congress. In short, rising discontent among the educated and partly educated urban middle class, as well as among the aspirants to middle-class occupations, exerted a destabilizing influence on Indian political parties in the mid 1970s.

[3] *Overseas Hindustan Times*, July 24, 1975.

After the 1972 elections Congress also began to lose support among what is often described as the unorganized or informal service sector of the urban economy—washermen, domestic servants, hawkers, peddlers, newspaper sellers, and rickshaw pullers, who earn their livings largely by providing services to the urban middle classes and who live in makeshift accommodations adjoining the middle-class neighborhoods they service. Since they depend for their income upon the middle class, when middle-class income declines in a period of inflation this low-income service sector is badly hit. Though this class is not organized into trade unions or associations, it is often drawn into the political arena by political parties seeking participation for public demonstrations and agitation. This group, which gave public support to Indira Gandhi in the 1969 split, was reported to have participated in agitation against the prime minister and against the state Congress party leaders in Bihar and Gujarat in 1974 and 1975.[4]

But Congress was not doing well in the rural areas either. The Congress party's base among the rural elite was no longer secure. Local rural elites remained anxious over the central government's threat to impose ceilings on landholding. And many rural Congressmen of local standing were disgruntled at the central government's intervention in the choice of state leaders, which deprived them of influence at the state level. Finally, at a time when the children of peasant proprietors were entering secondary schools and colleges in an effort to join the urban middle class, the growth of urban unemployment seriously affected the mobility of India's rural gentry.

Nor had the prime minister succeeded in compensating for the loss of these middle sectors by attracting support from the lower-income groups. With two successive years of poor rainfall, a drop in food grain production, a rise in food prices, growth in rural unemployment, a recession in the industrial sector, and increased retrenchment, there was hardly any improvement for either the urban or the rural poor.

Even before the emergency was declared, therefore, it was evident that the popular base of the Congress party had declined in both the cities and the countryside. Though the obvious differences between rural and urban India would lead one to expect rural voters to differ in their political outlooks from more affluent and educated urban voters, the urban-rural political cleavage is not strong here. In fact, there are many ties between urban and rural India and many common influences at work. Rural dwellers have extensive contact

---

[4] See Ghanshyam Shah, "Revolution, Reform, or Protest?" *Economic and Political Weekly*, April 16, 1977.

with urban areas; urban migrants regularly return to their rural homes; many of India's secondary school and college students living in towns and cities come from rural areas where they continue to maintain ties; school teachers, lawyers, and bureaucrats work in the countryside as well as in the towns and cities; and paved roads, transistor radios, the regional language press, and the bus system are part of a communications and transportation network linking rural and urban India.

Most important, the party system penetrates rural as well as urban areas. Congress party organizations are found all over India, and so are the organizations of the numerous opposition parties. Party workers can be found in the villages, often playing an important role in linking them not only to the party but to the state administrative machinery.

It is now quite clear that many features of the emergency were as irritating to rural as to urban Indians and that brutalities experienced in one center, rural or urban, were soon known over long distances, even in the absence of a free press. The bulldozing of slum dwellings in Delhi, for example, had repercussions in villages in northern India where many of the slum dwellers had relatives. Similarly, word of the sterilization program spread from one Muslim or Harijan community to another and between urban and rural centers. The shootings at Turkman Gate in Delhi were soon known to Muslims elsewhere in northern India. The fact that news of such events was suppressed by government censors may have even led to its exaggeration.

Arbitrary government officials were no less arbitrary in the country than in the cities, and people everywhere evidently recognized that the decline of the elected official made them vulnerable to arbitrary authority. Even government by corrupt elected officials was preferable to the authoritarian regime under which they lived during the emergency.

Reserved Constituencies

More than a fifth of India's parliamentary constituencies (116 of the 520) are reserved for members of "scheduled" castes or tribes.[5] Scheduled castes—they are variously known as Harijans and ex-untouchables—are among India's lowest-income groups. They are scat-

---

[5] Harijans and tribals are called "scheduled" because they are recorded on a government list or schedule. Members of castes and tribes listed on the schedule are entitled to various government benefits, including quotas for admission to college and civil service jobs. According to the 1971 census, 14.6 percent of India's population belonged to scheduled castes.

tered throughout the country but tend to be highly concentrated in sections of Uttar Pradesh (where 21 percent of the population belong to scheduled castes), West Bengal (20 percent), Tamil Nadu (18 percent), Haryana (19 percent), Punjab (22 percent), Himachal Pradesh (23 percent), Rajasthan (17 percent), Bihar (14 percent), Orissa (16 percent), and Madhya Pradesh (13 percent).

The Election Commission has reserved seventy-eight parliamentary constituencies for scheduled-caste candidates; in these constituencies only members of scheduled castes can stand, though the entire population can vote. Since the electorates in these constituencies are only partially made up of scheduled-caste voters, one should be careful not to infer that the outcomes only reflect the preferences of the scheduled castes. Nonetheless it is interesting to see whether the voting patterns in these constituencies differ markedly from voting patterns elsewhere.

In the 1977 elections Congress put up candidates for seventy-one of the seventy-eight seats and won sixteen, or 20 percent, of the seats; Janata ran fifty-nine candidates and won forty-five victories (58 percent; see Table 10). The Congress victories were primarily in Andhra, Karnataka, Maharashtra, and Tamil Nadu, that is, the states where Congress did well generally. Similarly, the Janata party swept the scheduled-caste seats in the northern states. In Bihar, the home

TABLE 10

ELECTION RESULTS IN SCHEDULED-CASTE CONSTITUENCIES, 1971 AND 1977

| | 1971 | | | 1977 | | |
| | | Seats won | | | Seats won | |
Party	Seats contested	Number	%	Seats contested	Number	%
Congress	66	50	64	71	16	20
"Janata party"	109	8	10	59	45	58
CPI	11	3	4	8	2	3
CPM	15	6	8	9	6	8
Other parties	50	10	13	21	7	9
Independents	102	1	1	91	2	3
Total	353	78	100	259	78	101

NOTE: The number of independent candidates may not be accurate. Some independents withdrew too late to have their names removed from the ballot. Others were the candidates of local parties that were too small to receive recognition by the Election Commission. In any event, the number of votes received by most independent candidates was very small, often only 1 or 2 percent of the total vote. SOURCE: See Table 3.

state of Jagjivan Ram, India's most prominent Harijan leader, Congress did worse in five of the scheduled-caste constituencies than in the state as a whole but fared somewhat better than average in three of the constituencies. Janata did better than its state-wide average in seven of these eight constituencies. In the eighteen constituencies reserved for scheduled castes in Uttar Pradesh, Congress did worse in fifteen than in the state as a whole. However, in the five reserved seats in Madhya Pradesh, in two of the four in Rajasthan, and in three of the five in Haryana and Punjab, Congress did somewhat better than in the state as a whole, though Congress lost all of these seats. On balance, then, in the country as a whole Congress failed to hold the Harijan reserved seats in spite of an earlier record of Congress victories. In 1971, Congress had won fifty of the sixty-six reserved seats it had contested, or 64 percent of all reserved constituencies.

Tribal populations are the other group with reserved constituencies.[6] India's 38 million tribals (1971 census) constitute only 6.9 percent of the population but they are so concentrated that they actually constitute a majority of the population in several parts of the country. Tribes form a majority in three states, all located in the northeast: Nagaland (89 percent), Meghalaya (80 percent), and Arunachal Pradesh (79 percent); in addition, they are a majority in nineteen districts in other states, three in Orissa, six in Madhya Pradesh, two in Himachal Pradesh, one in Bihar, two in Rajasthan, two in Assam, two in Gujarat, and one in the Laccadive Islands. In another nineteen districts they constitute more than 30 percent of the population.

The Election Commission reserved thirty-eight parliamentary constituencies for tribals; in addition may be counted the constituencies in Nagaland (one) and Meghalaya (two) which, though they are not reserved, have overwhelmingly tribal populations and are invariably contested by tribals.

Congress won thirteen (34 percent) of the constituencies reserved for tribals, while Janata won twenty (53 percent), as against twenty-six and five respectively in the 1971 parliamentary elections (see Table 11). Congress also won one of the seats in Meghalaya (an independent won the other), while a regional party won the Nagaland seat.

Though Congress lost most of the reserved tribal seats, it actu-

---

[6] For a more detailed account of the demography of India's tribals and their voting patterns for state assembly elections, see Myron Weiner and John Osgood Field, "How Tribal Constituencies in India Vote," in Myron Weiner and John Osgood Field, eds., *Electoral Politics in the Indian States: Three Disadvantaged Sectors*, vol. 2 (New Delhi: Manohar Book Service, 1975), pp. 79–199.

TABLE 11
ELECTION RESULTS IN SCHEDULED TRIBAL CONSTITUENCIES, 1971 AND 1977

	1971			1977		
		Seats won			Seats won	
Party	Seats contested	Number	%	Seats contested	Number	%
Congress	33	26	70	38	13	34
"Janata party"	45	5	14	30	20	53
CPM	5	1	3	4	3	8
Other parties	18	2	5	3	1	3
Independents	56	3	8	36	1	3
Total	157	37	100	111	38	101

SOURCE: See Table 3.

ally did better in these constituencies than in the states in which they were located in twenty-two instances and fared worse in fourteen—as compared with fifteen and fourteen respectively for the Janata party.

But again, the major finding is that tribal constituencies tended to vote same way as the states in which they were located. In Andhra (the only state in south India with tribal constituencies) the two reserved tribal constituencies elected Congressmen, while in the three Hindi states with tribal constituencies Janata won fifteen of sixteen seats. As in previous elections tribal constituencies were more like the nontribal constituencies of the state in which they were located than they were like tribal constituencies in other states. They were part of the mainstream.

Turnout

In 1977 60.5 percent of India's electorate voted, or 193.7 million out of a total electorate of 320 million. The registration of voters is the responsibility not of individual citizens but of the Election Commission, which prepares the electoral rolls through a house-to-house canvass. All citizens twenty-one years of age or older are registered. There are no literacy, educational, or property requirements.

The turnout was well above the 55.3 percent who took part in the 1971 parliamentary elections that swept Indira Gandhi back into power, but slightly short of the record turnout of 61.3 percent in the 1967 general elections (see Table 12).

The increase in voter turnout was particularly great in the states

TABLE 12
Voter Turnout, by State, 1971 and 1977
(in percentages and percentage points)

State	1971	1977	Change in Turnout	Change in Congress Vote
Andhra Pradesh	59.1	62.4	+ 3.3	+ 1.6
Assam	50.7	55.0	+ 4.3	− 6.4
Bihar	49.0	61.1	+12.1	−17.2
Gujarat	55.5	59.2	+ 3.7	+ 1.6
Haryana	64.4	73.3	+ 8.9	−34.6
Himachal Pradesh	41.2	61.5	+20.3	−38.7
Jammu and Kashmir	58.1	57.6	− 0.5	−38.7
Karnataka	57.4	63.0	+ 5.6	−14.0
Kerala	64.5	79.1	+14.6	+ 9.3
Madhya Pradesh	48.0	54.9	+ 6.9	−13.0
Maharashtra	59.9	60.9	+ 1.0	−16.5
Manipur	48.9	60.2	+11.3	+15.2
Nagaland	53.8	52.8	− 1.0	+ 7.1
Orissa	43.2	44.7	+ 1.5	− 0.2
Punjab	59.9	73.4	+13.5	−10.0
Rajasthan	54.0	56.9	+ 2.9	−19.7
Tamil Nadu	71.8	68.9	− 2.9	+ 9.8
Tripura	60.8	70.1	+ 9.3	+ 3.4
Uttar Pradesh	46.1	56.5	+10.4	−23.0
West Bengal	61.9	60.2	− 1.7	+ 4.0
Delhi	65.2	71.4	+ 6.2	−34.3
Total, India	55.3	60.5	+ 5.2	− 9.1

Source: See Table 2.

which had been hit hard by the government's sterilization program—
Bihar, Haryana, Himachal Pradesh, Punjab, and Uttar Pradesh.[7] In
Haryana and the Punjab, the two states surrounding the capital city,
resentment of the sterilization program was particularly intense. In the
Punjab 73 percent of the voters went to the polls, about thirteen per-
centage points more than in the previous election.

[7] According to David Gwatkin of the Overseas Development Council, the sterilization rate in Uttar Pradesh (U.P.) was actually lower than that of other states
in India, though high compared with U.P.'s own past performance. U.P. performed 6.5 times as many sterilizations in 1976–1977 as in the previous year, a
rate of increase twice that of the rest of India. "It seems to me reasonable," he
writes, in a letter to the author, "that such a rapid acceleration starting from
the unusually low base represented by U.P.'s miserable past performance should
lead to the intense popular reaction against family planning observed, even
though the 1976–1977 U.P. performance wasn't all that high relative to that of
other states in that year."

Three states which did not experience the worst excesses of the sterilization program but nonetheless gave the opposition an overwhelming majority of seats, showed little or no increase in turnout—West Bengal, Orissa, and Rajasthan. It is worth noting that of these only Rajasthan actually registered a massive voter swing against Congress.

There were increases in voter turnout in the south as well, but smaller than those in the northern states that voted against Congress. The turnouts in Andhra and Karnataka, though higher than in 1971, were well below those of most of the northern states, and in Tamil Nadu turnout actually declined. Only in Kerala was there a substantial increase in the proportion of voters.

In all there were eleven states where the increase in turnout exceeded the 5.2 percentage point nationwide increase over 1971, and in eight of these Congress declined by 10 to 39 percentage points. Congress did better only in three, the small states of Kerala, Manipur, and Tripura. In ten states the turnout either rose by less than the nationwide average or declined; the Congress vote increased in five of these and declined in the other five, in Jammu and Kashmir, Maharashtra, and Rajasthan by significant margins.

The election returns thus confirmed the widespread impression that the emergency, rather than reducing the politicization of the country, actually increased it. People who had not taken part in the previous election—whether new younger voters or older persons who had not voted before we cannot say—came out to vote, and it would appear that most of them voted against the government.

Some of the largest increases in voter turnout were in the reserved scheduled-caste constituencies.[8] In the 1971 elections the difference between the turnout in scheduled-caste constituencies and that in the state as a whole was —7.0 percentage points in Uttar Pradesh, —5.6 in Bihar, —5.8 in Rajasthan, —5.5 in Haryana, —2.9 in Himachal Pradesh, —3.9 in Madhya Pradesh, and —2.1 in the Punjab. In 1977 the difference was —2.0 percentage points in Uttar Pradesh, +2.5 in Bihar, —1.6 in Rajasthan, —0.3 in Haryana, —2.8 in Himachal Pradesh, +1.2 in Madhya Pradesh, and +0.5 in Punjab. In other words, the turnout in these forty-one scheduled-caste constituencies in the north increased by a great deal more than in the general constituencies. Moreover, in Bihar and Madhya Pradesh the average turnout in scheduled-caste constituencies actually exceeded that of the state as a whole (see Table 13).

---

[8] No comparable change in turnout appears to have taken place in the scheduled-tribe constituencies. Their turnout increased, but no more than that of the general constituencies in their states.

TABLE 13

Voter Turnout in Scheduled-Caste Constituencies Compared with State-wide Turnout, by State, 1971 and 1977

State[a]	1971		1977	
	Turnout	Difference	Turnout	Difference
Uttar Pradesh	46.1		56.5	
Uttar Pradesh sc (18)	39.1	−7.0	54.5	−2.0
Bihar	49.0		61.1	
Bihar sc (8)	43.4	−5.6	63.6	+2.5
Tamil Nadu	71.8		68.9	
Tamil Nadu sc (7)	73.5	+1.7	68.4	−0.5
Rajasthan	54.0		56.9	
Rajasthan sc (4)	48.2	−5.8	55.3	−1.6
Andhra Pradesh	59.1		62.4	
Andhra Pradesh sc (6)	56.2	−2.9	60.0	−2.4
Karnataka	57.4		63.0	
Karnataka sc (4)	57.1	−0.3	59.2	−3.8
Haryana	64.4		73.3	
Haryana sc (2)	58.9	−5.5	73.0	−0.3
Himachal Pradesh	41.2		61.5	
Himachal Pradesh sc (1)	38.3	−2.9	58.7	−2.8
Madhya Pradesh	48.0		54.9	
Madhya Pradesh sc (5)	44.1	−3.9	56.1	+1.2
West Bengal	61.9		60.2	
West Bengal sc (8)	63.6	+1.7	60.4	+0.2
Punjab	59.9		73.4	
Punjab sc (3)	57.8	−2.1	73.9	+0.5

[a] The number of scheduled-caste constituencies in each state is in parentheses; sc stands for scheduled caste.
SOURCE: See Table 2.

As one might expect, no such change occurred in the scheduled-caste constituencies in Andhra, Tamil Nadu, and Karnataka. In these states the gap remained and in the last two it grew. Here again we have circumstantial evidence suggesting that the emergency politicized the lowest-income groups in northern, but not southern, India and that a considerable portion of the vote against the Congress party and for Janata came from new voters in these low-income groups.

7

The Elections and the Party System

A Two-Party System?

The elections brought to an end the "Congress system," under which one party, made up of conflicting factions, had dominated the national government of India and most of the states for thirty years. The numerous opposition groups, alone, in concert, or in alliance with factions of the governing party, had sometimes made inroads into individual states, but they had never shared power at the national level.

In its place does India now have a two-party system? Given the newness of the Janata party as well as the fragility of the Congress party in the wake of defeat, it is premature to conclude that India now has a stable two-party system. Nonetheless, it is clear that the elections consolidated the electorate into two camps. In the 1971 elections Congress won 43.6 percent of the vote while the nearest opposition, the Congress O., won only slightly more than 10 percent; Jana Sangh took 7 percent. Congress held two-thirds of the seats in Parliament, and no opposition group had the fifty M.P.s necesary to be declared an official parliamentary opposition.

In the 1977 elections Congress and Janata together won 78 percent of the vote and 83 percent of the seats in Parliament (see Table 13). Moreover, the electoral polarization involved more than simply the consolidation of many opposition parties into the Janata party, for the combined two-party vote in 1977 exceeded what it would have been in 1971 had all the constituents of Janata then been joined into a single party. Today, only eighty-eight members of Parliament (who together polled 16 percent of the vote) are independents or belong to other parties.

A two-party system—for present purposes, one in which two parties share at least 80 percent of the total vote—now operates at the parliamentary level in twelve of the seventeen states that elect more than two members to Parliament (see Table 14). (Five small states elect only one or two M.P.s.) These twelve are Andhra, Assam, Bihar, Gujarat, Haryana, Himachal, Karnataka, Madhya Pradesh, Maharashtra, Orissa, Rajasthan, and Uttar Pradesh. In addition, the union territory of Delhi (with seven parliamentary seats) gave the two parties 98 percent of the vote. These states contain 75 percent of India's electorate.

The Multiparty States. Five states still have multiparty systems—Jammu and Kashmir, Kerala, Punjab, Tamil Nadu, and West Bengal. They contain 23 percent of the electorate.

In Jammu and Kashmir the party system revolves around the National Conference, led by Sheikh Abdullah. In the 1971 elections it threw its weight behind Indira Gandhi's Congress, but it has since reemerged as an independent political force (see Table 15).

TABLE 14
TWO-PARTY VOTE ("JANATA" PLUS CONGRESS), BY STATE, 1971 AND 1977
(in percentages and percentage points)

State	1971	1977	Change
Andhra Pradesh	67.9	89.7	+21.8
Assam	68.6	86.4	+17.8
Bihar	74.1	87.9	+13.8
Gujarat	93.9	96.4	+ 0.5
Haryana	78.2	88.4	+10.2
Himachal Pradesh	94.7	96.7	+ 2.0
Jammu and Kashmir	67.0	29.0	−38.0
Karnataka	95.0	96.7	+ 1.7
Kerala	25.9	36.3	+10.4
Madhya Pradesh	84.2	90.5	+ 6.3
Maharashtra	76.0	80.2	+ 4.2
Manipur	44.3	53.9	+ 9.6
Nagaland	39.5	46.6	+ 7.1
Orissa	89.0	90.0	+ 1.0
Punjab	55.8	48.9	− 6.9
Rajasthan	81.6	95.8	+14.2
Tamil Nadu	53.2	38.4	−14.8
Tripura	36.8	57.5	+20.7
Uttar Pradesh	86.0	93.0	+ 7.0
West Bengal	40.6	53.2	+12.6
Delhi	95.9	98.4	+ 2.5
Total, India	71.3	77.7	+ 6.4

SOURCE: See Table 2.

TABLE 15

ELECTION RETURNS IN MULTIPARTY STATES, 1971 AND 1977
(in percentages)

State and Party	1971	1977
Jammu and Kashmir		
Congress	53.9	15.2
Janata	13.1	13.8
National Conference	—	35.0
Independents	32.2	41.3
Kerala		
Congress	19.8	29.1
Janata	6.1	7.2
CPI	9.1	10.4
CPM	26.2	20.4
Others	20.8	24.3
Punjab		
Congress	45.9	35.8
Janata	9.9	13.0
Akali Dal	30.8	40.5
Tamil Nadu		
Congress	12.5	22.3
Janata	40.7	16.1
DMK	35.3	19.6
AIADMK	—	30.6
West Bengal		
Congress	27.7	31.7
Janata	12.9	21.5
CPI	10.3	4.2
CPM	34.5	26.2

SOURCE: See Table 3.

In Kerala the two Communist parties together tend to win a third of the electorate. Kerala also has several small regional parties including the Muslim League, a remnant of the preindependence party, which continues to exercise a hold among Kerala's Muslim community; the splinter Muslim League Opposition; and Kerala Congress, a split-off from the Congress party.

In the Punjab it is the Shiromani Akali Dal, with its powerful social base in the Sikh religious community, that forms the centerpin of the party system. In the 1977 elections this group was allied with Janata, but in the previous election it had thrown its weight—generally a third or so of the electorate—behind Congress.

Similarly, in Tamil Nadu, as we have seen, two regional parties, the Dravida Munnetra Kazhagam (DMK) and the All India Anna DMK, dominate the political system. Together they won half the vote in the 1977 elections, while Congress and Janata won only 38 percent. The party scene in this state is particularly fluid; the DMK again split after its defeat in the parliamentary elections, while the Janata party shifted its alliance from the DMK to the AIADMK.

Finally, in West Bengal the two Communist parties are significant elements in the party system. The CPI, which tied itself closely to the Congress party, was virtually wiped out as a significant political force, but the CPM continues to be a major force in the state. The total CPM vote declined in the 1977 parliamentary elections, but the party contested fewer constituencies and won a larger vote per seat than in the 1971 elections.[1] The CPM won eighteen of the twenty-one constituencies it contested, as compared with twenty of thirty-eight in 1971. In state assembly elections held in June 1977 the CPM emerged as the largest force in the state assembly and subsequently replaced the Congress government.

The Communist Parties. The two Communist parties, the CPI and the CPM, are now the only two national opposition parties that have not merged with either Congress or Janata. But they are national only in ambition and in the fact that the Election Commission recognizes them as such. In political reality, they are only a significant force in a few regions.

Nationally, the Communist parties declined from forty-eight seats in 1971 (twenty-three CPI, twenty-five CPM) to only twenty-eight seats in the new Parliament (seven CPI, twenty-one CPM). They dropped from 9 percent of the vote to 7.1 percent. Of the two parties, the CPM suffered less, since it had been opposed to the emergency and had allied itself with the Janata party. The CPI had supported the government, and its alliance with Congress cost it seats and votes everywhere outside Kerala (see Tables 16 and 17).

Neither party now counts nationally as an electoral force, though the CPI continues its efforts to find allies within the major parties. In the past it closely allied itself with "progressive" elements in the Congress party, and it seems likely that it will now seek to tie itself with "progressive" members of the Janata party, particularly in Uttar Pradesh, Bihar, and Orissa where it has ties with a number of former Congressmen and women who have become members of Janata governments. Electorally the CPI continues to be a significant

---

[1] In 1971 the CPM secured an average of 118,000 votes per parliamentary candidate in West Bengal, as against 192,000 in 1977. Janata, which won all twelve of the seats it contested in West Bengal in 1977, won the highest average of votes per seat, 215,000.

TABLE 16

COMMUNIST PARTY OF INDIA VOTE, BY STATE, 1971 AND 1977
(in percentages and percentage points)

State	1971	1977	Change
Andhra Pradesh	5.9	2.7	—3.2
Assam	5.6	1.4	—4.2
Bihar	9.9	5.6	—4.3
Kerala	9.1	10.4	+1.3
Madhya Pradesh	1.1	0.5	—0.6
Maharashtra	1.7	0.7	—1.0
Manipur	15.0	11.5	—3.5
Orissa	4.3	3.2	—1.1
Punjab	6.2	1.6	—4.6
Tamil Nadu	5.4	4.6	—0.8
Tripura	6.8	.0	—6.8
Uttar Pradesh	4.4	1.1	—3.3
West Bengal	10.3	4.2	—6.1
Total, India	4.8	2.8	—2.0

NOTE: All of the states in which the Communist party of India ran candidates are shown. For the distribution of CPI seats in Parliament see Tables 4 and 5.
SOURCE: See Table 3.

TABLE 17

COMMUNIST PARTY OF INDIA (MARXIST) VOTE, BY STATE, 1971 AND 1977
(in percentages and percentage points)

State	1971	1977	Change
Andhra Pradesh	2.8	4.7	+1.9
Assam	1.4	2.9	+1.5
Kerala	26.2	20.4	—5.8
Maharashtra	0.5	3.6	+3.1
Orissa	1.1	2.0	+0.9
Punjab	2.2	5.1	+2.9
Tamil Nadu	1.6	1.6	0
Tripura	43.5	34.1	—9.4
West Bengal	34.5	26.2	—8.3
Total, India	5.2	4.3	—0.9

NOTE: All of the states where the Communist party Marxist ran candidates are shown. Tripura, where the CPM won its highest percentage in both years, has only two seats in the national Parliament. For the distribution of CPM seats in Parliament see Tables 4 and 5.
SOURCE: See Table 3.

force in Kerala and in the small northeastern state of Manipur. Once a major power in West Bengal, it failed to win a single seat there in the 1977 elections.

The CPM, by freeing itself from its associations with the Soviet Union and an unpopular Congress government, has improved its political prospects as an independent leftist force. It has a substantial following among both the urban middle class and sections of the industrial labor force in Kerala, West Bengal, and the small northeastern state of Tripura.

Twenty of the twenty-eight seats won by the two Communist parties were from Kerala and West Bengal. The CPI lost its growing base in Bihar, where it had captured a tenth of the vote in 1971 and five of the state's fifty-three seats; this time it won no seats, and its vote dropped to only 5.6 percent. Its efforts to build a rural base in the state have been thwarted. Similarly, it failed to hold its once significant rural base in Andhra.

In contrast, the CPM has been able to sustain a small rural base in a few constituencies in Andhra (it won approximately one-third of the vote in five rural constituencies), but it too has a disproportionate share of its strength in urban constituencies. At the moment both parties seem regionally trapped and without a significant political base in any areas outside Kerala, West Bengal, and Tripura, though they have pockets of support in Maharashtra, Punjab, Andhra, and Bihar.

Regional Parties. The regional parties are the wild cards in Indian politics. While they may win only a tenth or so of the vote nationally and less than fifty seats in Parliament, they are a persistent and important force in a number of states. In some states, as we have seen, the regional parties are institutionally part of the local party system. In Tamil Nadu, for example, the DMK is a well-established, socially rooted, historical force dating back in various guises to the 1920s. Now split into two political groups, the DMK represents Tamil nationalism, a non-Brahmin social base, antipathy to northern domination which is seen as Hindi "imperialism," and an egalitarian populist streak.

Similarly, in the Punjab the Akali Dal has deep roots in the Sikh community, strong ties to the Sikh temples, and a nationalist bent which forced the central government to carve a predominantly Sikh state out of the Punjab, leaving the remaining Hindu areas to form the separate state of Haryana.

Regional parties with strong social and emotional bases in their communities have been a feature of Indian politics since independence.

Some, like the Akali Dal, the DMK, the National Conference in Jammu and Kashmir, the Muslim League, and the parties in the tribal states of Nagaland and Manipur, are well established and have attracted the support of enough voters to make the political systems of the states where they are located distinctive. In other states short-lived regional parties have sprung up from time to time, exploiting specific grievances. Some of these ephemeral groups have demanded the rearrangement of state boundaries to coincide with linguistic borders. These regional parties were particularly active in the mid 1950s when there was widespread agitation for the creation of linguistic states. After the rearrangement of state boundaries in 1956 most of these groups merged with the national parties. Nevertheless, the intensity of regional attachments in much of India and the existence of complex layers of social and cultural identification, each of which can be tapped by political groups crusading for particular causes, mean that regional parties are likely to remain part of the political scene for a long time.

The Emergence of a New National Party

It is a formidable task for a national party to reach out across this vast country of over 600 million people speaking thirteen major and innumerable minor languages and impelled by an astonishing variety of economic and social interests. The success of the Congress party can be partly attributed to the unifying effects of the nationalist struggle against alien rulers, which cut across particularistic loyalties. After independence Congress succeeded where nationalist movements in other countries did not in holding its wildly diverse supporters together in a single political party that commanded support in villages and neighborhoods throughout the country. While other political groups, on the left and right, had national pretensions, none was able to create unity from diversity in the way that made the Congress party victorious. Congress maintained its support by developing a broad-gauged program intended to appeal to a multiplicity of interests, by keeping the party open to aspiring social groups seeking a share of power, by the effective use of patronage, and through the bargaining and balancing skills of its leadership. Consensual politics often produced Congress governments without definite policy priorities, reluctant to make strong decisions and implement policy firmly; it produced what Gunnar Myrdal in his book *The Asian Dilemma* called India's "soft state." Nevertheless it succeeded in keeping a mélange of interests within the Congress fold.

Like most nationalist movements in colonial countries, India's grew out of the struggle for independence. Democracy, though one of its objectives, was secondary, a British legacy valued more by the elite than by the masses. But the legacy proved durable, and as India's democratic institutions functioned through the 1950s and 1960s, political interests emerged that could only thrive in a democratic atmosphere. The press in India was free; countless political parties were accustomed to seeking public support; trade unions could strike; the courts could challenge the government; agrarian groups were organized to make claims upon government revenues; student and youth groups agitated in the schools and colleges; caste, tribal, linguistic, and religious associations sought to further the special interests of their communities. The suspension of free speech, freedom of assembly, and *habeas corpus* by Mrs. Gandhi's government took place not in a politically backward or chaotic ex-colony, but in a functioning democracy.

During the emergency groups with highly diverse economic interests, ethnic attachments, and ideological orientations came to recognize that they shared a concern with the preservation—or the reestablishment—of procedures under which they could freely deal with the public, with each other, and with those who exercised governmental authority. Political parties with national aspirations but regional bases of support looked up from their local concerns and united. What galvanized them—just as the fight for India's independence had earlier galvanized the groups that became the Congress party—was an immediate threat to their freedom. In an unexpected and ironic way, Mrs. Gandhi drew the opposition together and turned them into committed democrats.

If the campaign rhetoric of the opposition seems unoriginal to outsiders, it is because it consisted largely of the elementary principals of democracy—recited, however, with new conviction by people who had discovered afresh the price of arbitrary, tyrannical government, and the benefits of living in a free society under the rule of law. Values that had been learned in school took on new meaning: *habeas corpus* meant that you and your friends could not be summarily arrested; a free press meant that you could read about what was actually going on in your community and elsewhere in the country; freedom of assembly meant that you could meet with your fellow workers or neighbors when you shared grievances against your employer or against the government. During the emergency many of the long-term differences among political groups melted into unimportance compared with the loss of these fundamental rights. Members of the Jana Sangh who had been attracted to the notion of a strong centralized regime in a unified nationalist India were distressed by the centralized authoritarianism created by the prime minister. Socialists who had advocated a strong public sector and programs to aid low-income groups found that they rejected some of the measures passed by the Congress government in the name of egalitarian socialism. The party that emerged in the country's jails during the emergency pulled together workers from several political parties not simply on a program of bringing down Congress, but around a commitment to democratic values. It is impossible to foresee how long the Janata party will remain intact, but for the time being it seems clear that it is something more than a mere one-shot coalition.

India's emergent two-party system is polarized around two historic forces, one that emerged out of a nationalist struggle and another that emerged out of a democratic struggle. The Janata party may well be as nationalist as the Congress party (though some sections may be more tolerant of foreign investment), but it is likely to be more vigilant with respect to human rights and more supportive of an open political and economic marketplace. And for some time the Congress party, with or without Indira Gandhi, will carry the burden of responsibility for having led the country off in an authoritarian and centralist direction.

8

Epilogue

A Restoration Government

The first acts of the Janata government were to eliminate the repressive practices, laws, and administrative procedures that had been introduced during the emergency and to restore India's political institutions to their preemergency functions.[1] Indeed, many of the measures adopted by the new government were intended to restore practices and institutions that had fallen into disuse in the last few years of Mrs. Gandhi's tenure even before the declaration of the emergency. Censorship was ended and a commission was appointed to propose ways of making Samachar, the news agency formed in 1976 by the government out of four previously existing agencies, independent of government. The prime minister's secretariat, which had become a political arm of the prime minister and had grown independent of (and a rival to) the cabinet secretariat, was reorganized by Morarji Desai and restored to its pre-1964 position. The chief of the Research and Analysis Wing (RAW), the intelligence organization that provided the prime minister with political intelligence, resigned and was replaced by the head of the Intelligence Bureau, the agency normally responsible for political intelligence and internal security.[2] Six hundred officers of RAW were relieved of their duties and sent back to positions in the states. In various other departments and ministries officials

---

[1] Several issues of *Seminar* magazine provide detailed analyses of the post-election scene and contain some thoughtful reflections on the emergency, the elections, and the problems ahead. See the April 1977 issue on "The Elections and the System"; the May 1977 issue, "Correctives"; June 1977, "Atrocities"; July 1977, "Rethinking"; and August 1977, "Janata Phase." See also Girilal Jain, "The Process of Realignment: New Political Hopes and Calculations," *Times of India*, March 30, 1977.

[2] Inder Malhotra, "The Intelligence Agencies—Need for Effective Supervising," *Times of India*, April 14, 1977.

who had worked closely with the prime minister and her associates or were responsible for some of the worst excesses were also removed or transferred.

The government launched investigations into the alleged criminal activities of key associates of Indira Gandhi, and Bansi Lal, the former defense minister, and several others were subsequently arrested. A commission of inquiry was appointed, under former Supreme Court Chief Justice Shah, to conduct a wide-ranging inquiry into acts committed during the emergency.

Revenue intelligence, which had been effectively removed from the control of the finance minister and taken over by the prime minister's secretariat, resumed its normal functioning. The supersession of judges and other departures from established procedures for the appointment and transfer of judges came to an end. The new prime minister and his minister of health and family planning, Raj Narain (the man who had defeated Indira Gandhi at Rae Bareli), announced that the family planning program would continue since the country could not afford its present rate of population growth, but that there would be no compulsory sterilization.

Finally, the government declared its intention to rescind the Forty-Second Amendment and to remove from the Constitution article 352, which permits the government to proclaim an emergency without prior parliamentary approval.

Political Consolidation

The Council of Ministers appointed by Prime Minister Morarji Desai carefully reflected the various political forces that had banded together within the Janata party. Jagjivan Ram and H. N. Bahuguna, the leaders of the Congress for Democracy, which had merged with Janata, were brought into the cabinet. Charan Singh, the elder leader of the Bharatiya Lok Dal and a powerful figure in the politics of Uttar Pradesh, became home minister. Atal Behari Vajpayee, one-time leader of the Jana Sangh parliamentary party, was made minister of external affairs. H. M. Patel, a civil servant turned politician who had joined the Swatantra party, was made minister of finance. Mohan Dharia, a Young Turk who had resigned from the Congress party in support of Jayaprakash Narayan, was brought in to take charge of the ministry of commerce. George Fernandes, the Socialist trade unionist, was placed in charge of the ministry of industries. L. K. Advani, president of the Jana Sangh and on the eve of the elections general secretary of the Janata party, was appointed minister of information and broadcasting.

The Janata government brought together elder statesmen with years of experience as ministers in the states or in the central government and younger men with little or no governmental experience. Among the younger figures in the new government, each with an important power base of his own within the Janata party, were Vajpayee who was fifty-one, Dharia (fifty-two), Advani (fifty), and Fernandes (forty-seven). Conspicuously absent were any prominent figures from south India. The cabinet consisted primarily of leaders from Uttar Pradesh but included members from Bihar, Maharashtra, Gujarat, and Madhya Pradesh and a single figure from Kerala.

At the first postelection meeting of the Janata party, Chandra Shekhar, the forty-nine-year-old former Young Turk Congressman and one-time joint secretary of the Praja Socialist party in Uttar Pradesh, was elected president of the party. A close friend and admirer of Jayaprakash Narayan, Chandra Shekhar, had been instrumental in bringing the various parties together to form the Janata party early in the year.

In a second phase of consolidation, the new government announced that it was pressing the Congress governments in most of the north Indian states to resign and to hold new state elections. Charan Singh, the home minister, noted that in nine states the Congress party had won only 9 out of 300 parliamentary seats and that this unprecedented rejection of the governing party required new elections for state assemblies. He explained that the government had not called for elections in Maharashtra and other states where Congress had lost but had retained a solid following.

State elections were held in June 1977 in fourteen states and union territories—Uttar Pradesh, Bihar, Madhya Pradesh, West Bengal, Rajasthan, Orissa, Punjab, Haryana, Jammu and Kashmir, Goa, Himachal Pradesh, and Delhi, and in the south, Tamil Nadu (where elections were already overdue) and Pondicherry. In all, two-thirds of the country's electorate went to the polls.

The scramble for nominations threatened to tear the Janata party apart. Each group within the party demanded its fair share of seats. But in spite of these internal conflicts, the Janata wave against the Congress continued. Janata swept all but four of the states and the union territory of Pondicherry. It won an overwhelming 83 percent of the state assembly seats in Uttar Pradesh and Haryana, 66 percent in Bihar, 78 percent in Himachal, 72 percent in Madhya Pradesh, 75 percent in Orissa and Rajasthan, and 82 percent in Delhi. In West Bengal the Communist party Marxist won 61 percent of the seats with Janata backing. (For the results in number of seats see Table 18.)

Three other states chose regional parties to form governments:

TABLE 18

RESULTS OF STATE ASSEMBLY ELECTIONS, JUNE 1977

(in number of seats)

States	Total Seats	Janata	Con-gress	CPI	CPM	AIA-DMK	DMK	Other	Ind.
Bihar	324	214	57	21	4			5	22
Haryana	90	75	3					5	7
Himachal Pradesh	68	53	9						6
Madhya Pradesh	320	230	84						6
Jammu and Kashmir	76	13	11					45[a]	4
Orissa	147	110	26	1	1				9
Punjab	117	24	17	7	8			58[b]	2
Rajasthan	200	150	41	1	1				6
Tamil Nadu	234	10	27	5	12	130	48	1	1
Uttar Pradesh	424	351	46	9	1				16
West Bengal	294	29	20	2	178			55[c]	9
Delhi	56	46	10						
Pondicherry	30	7	2	1		14	3		3
Goa	30	3	10					15[d]	2

NOTE: There is a slight disparity in several states between the total seats and the declared results since polling in some constituencies was countermanded by the Election Commission.
[a] National Conference, 45 seats.
[b] Akali Dal, 58 seats.
[c] Revolutionary Socialist party 20 seats, Forward Bloc 25 (both leftist parties).
[d] Maharastrawadi Gomantas (a regional party confined to Goa), 15 seats.
SOURCE: See Table 3.

the Akali Dal in the Punjab, with nearly 50 percent of the seats, was allied with Janata (which won 20 percent of the seats); in Tamil Nadu the AIADMK, which had won almost half of the state's seats in the national Parliament, took 56 percent of the seats in the state assembly (it won slightly less in neighboring Pondicherry); and Jammu and Kashmir gave nearly 60 percent of its assembly seats to the National Conference.

In each state that Janata lost, it was a regional party or the Communists rather than Congress that formed the state government. Of India's eighteen major states and union territories (excluding for this purpose those with populations of less than 1 million) the Janata party controlled nine, containing 51 percent of the country's population, Congress controlled four and shared power in a fifth with 29 percent of the population, and the Communist party Marxist or regional parties controlled four, with another 19 percent of the population.

With this much variety among the state governments, the central government was no longer in a position to dictate policies to the states or to obtain the selection of pliant chief ministers. In fact, in an effort to demonstrate the autonomy of even the state Janata parties, the central government announced that the choice of chief ministers in states with Janata governments would be left entirely in the hands of the Janata members of the state legislative assemblies; the central party organization would not intervene. In four contiguous states— Haryana, Uttar Pradesh, Bihar, and Orissa—leaders of the former BLD took control; in Delhi, Himachal Pradesh, Rajasthan, and Madhya Pradesh, the former Jana Sangh took control of the chief ministerships. Socialist followers of Jayaprakash Narayan were contenders in Uttar Pradesh and Himachal, while in Rajasthan and Bihar, Morarji's old Congress O. unsuccessfully fought for control. In addition, therefore, to contending with state governments controlled by regional parties or by Congress, the Janata government may also find its former Socialist and Congress O. members in the central government clashing with some of their own state governments.

A month after the state assembly elections in June, new elections were held for the president of India, to fill the vacancy left by the incumbent's death in February. India's president—a constitutional, largely ceremonial head of state with political powers only when there is no parliamentary majority—is chosen by an electoral college consisting of members of Parliament (both the Lok Sabha and the Rajya Sabha[3]) and members of the state legislatures. In an effort to win the support of the regional parties and to reassert the nonpolitical status of the president, the Janata party sought the support of all groups, including Congress, for a consensus candidate. The sixty-four-year-old Neelam Sanjiva Reddi, speaker of the Lok Sabha and a prominent Janata leader from south India, was chosen. Ironically, Reddi had been the Congress party nominee in 1969 and had been defeated after Prime Minister Gandhi withdrew her support. His unanimous election to the presidency suggested a conciliation that was welcome even to members of the Congress party.

The Two Faces of Congress

Shorn of power in the central government and in all but four state governments (Maharashtra, Andhra Pradesh, Assam, and Karnataka),

---

[3] In addition to the Lok Sabha, the lower house elected by popular vote, India's Parliament includes the Rajya Sabha, an upper house whose members are chosen by the state legislatures. Besides forming part of the electoral college that chooses India's president, the Rajya Sabha plays a significant role in voting on constitutional amendments.

the Congress party became the leading opposition party. Congress-men who had spent their careers in political office were now out of power. Many resigned from the party and sought admission to the Janata party. A wave of recrimination swept the party leadership and the rank and file as losers and survivors alike sought to cast blame for the party's debacle and to find ways to recoup. Indira Gandhi's opponents blamed her, Sanjay, Bansi Lal, Shukla, and their associates, while her supporters attempted to diffuse the blame more broadly. D. K. Borooah, the Congress president, resigned his office. Bansi Lal was expelled from the party. A reprimand for "misuse of power" was given to V. C. Shukla, who had lost his parliamentary seat in Madhya Pradesh by one of the largest margins in the state. Y. B. Chavan, one of the leading survivors, was elected leader of the Congress parlia-mentary party.

Indira Gandhi's supporters argued that they should not join with Janata in defaming the party leadership, nor should they repudiate the emergency or the policies pursued by the party because of the excesses committed by a few. A battle soon ensued between the two groups over the office of Congress party president. Opponents of Mrs. Gandhi backed Siddharta Shankar Ray, chief minister of West Bengal and a one-time close associate of the prime minister who had turned against her when her son had attempted to undermine his position in the state. Mrs. Gandhi's supporters backed Brahmananda Reddy, her home minister. In the bitterly contested election in the All India Congress Committee, the party's governing council, Reddy won by 317 to 160 votes. Mrs. Gandhi thus demonstrated her continued popularity within the Congress party. Moreover, even as some party leaders were demoted, expelled, or reprimanded, no action was taken against Sanjay Gandhi, the person whom even Mrs. Gandhi's supporters held re-sponsible for the worst features of the emergency.

Though Congress was again defeated in the June 1977 state assembly elections, Congress leaders found consolation in the fact that this defeat was not as severe as that sustained in the parliamen-tary elections. Moreover, many Congress leaders continued to hope that as differences erupted within the state Janata party organizations over the next few years, the state Congress organizations would welcome defectors back into their fold. Many of the leftists within Congress also believed that internal "contradictions" within both Janata and Congress would eventually fragment the two parties and lead to a realignment that would benefit the left.

By the middle of 1977 Mrs. Gandhi was making statements to the press and attending party meetings. Her reentry into the political arena spurred Morarji Desai and Chandra Sekhar in their efforts to keep together the diverse elements within the Janata party. By the end of the year the struggle between Mrs. Gandhi and her opponents within Congress became acute. Her supporters attempted to dislodge Brahmananda Reddy and make Mrs. Gandhi the Congress president. When this failed Mrs. Gandhi and her supporters met in early January 1978 to form a party of their own, the Congress (I) (for Indira). Immediately at stake was who would win the March 1978 elections for state assemblies in Assam, Maharashtra, Andhra, and Karnataka, the four states remaining under Congress control. But what was at stake in the long run was what kind of Congress party would be the leading opposition to the Janata government: a Congress led by Mrs. Gandhi that had not repudiated the emergency, injecting a Bonapartist element into Indian politics, or a reformed Congress that repudiated the past.

The March elections showed that Mrs. Gandhi remained a popular political leader (see Table 19). The Congress (I) swept the polls in the two southern states. In Karnataka the Congress (I) won 149 of 224 seats, against 59 for the Janata party and only 2 seats for the Congress party led by Brahmananda Reddy. In nearby Andhra, the Congress (I) captured 175 out of the 293 state assembly seats, while the state Congress won only 30 seats, falling behind Janata which won 60 seats. No party won a majority of seats in either Maharashtra or Assam, but Janata emerged as the largest party in each, with the Congress coming in second and Congress (I) third. Brahmananda Reddy resigned as president of the Congress while Mrs. Gandhi declared that her victories in the south demonstrated that hers was the authentic Congress. In Kerala, several Congress assembly members

TABLE 19

RESULTS OF STATE ASSEMBLY ELECTIONS, MARCH 1978
(in number of seats)

State	Total Seats	Janata	Con-gress	Con-gress (I)	CPI	CPM	Other	Ind.
Andhra	293	60	30	175	5	8		15
Assam	126	53	26	8	5	11	11	12
Karnataka	224	59	2	149	3		11	
Maharashtra	288	99	69	62	1	9	29	19
Meghalaya	60		20				30	10

SOURCE: *India News* (Information Service, Embassy of India, Washington, D.C.), vol. 16, no. 50 (March 6, 1978), p. 7.

crossed the floor to join the former prime minister's party, leaving the Congress coalition government with a weakened majority. Would there now be similar defections to the Congress (I) elsewhere in the country?

Some observers expect the Janata party to assume the central role in the Indian political system once held by Congress. They see Janata as representing a plurality of interests and ideological strands, much like the Congress party of old, with a hold both in the cities and in the countryside. Moreover, they see it as attracting those who expect government to operate by patronage as well as those who seek ideological commitment. If they are right, Janata will remain intact and Congress, united or fragmented, will shrink into a small opposition force whose strength rests largely on alliances with dissident factions within Janata, much as in the past various opposition parties derived strength from alliances with factions of the Congress party.

For several reasons it is premature to assume that Congress dominance will simply be replaced by Janata dominance. For one thing, Janata still remains primarily a north Indian party. It has failed to win elections in any of the four southern states and holds only a plurality in Assam and Maharashtra, while other parties control West Bengal, Punjab, and Kashmir. Moreover, it is premature to assume that Congress, alone or divided, has no electoral strength of its own capable of threatening Janata control in the next parliamentary or state assembly elections. Congress did, after all, win 34.5 percent of the vote in the parliamentary elections and has continued to win a substantial share of the vote in state assembly elections held since March 1977, with Mrs. Gandhi's new Congress (I) doing well not only in the south but in several state assembly and parliamentary by-elections in the north as well.

For another, the loyalty of various groups within Janata is precarious; with an elderly, divided leadership at the national level, a restive younger leadership waiting in the wings, acute factional struggles in several of the north Indian Janata state governments, and a resurgent Congress (I), it is at least as possible that Janata dissidents will defect to one of the Congress parties as that Congressmen will defect to Janata in some of the states in northern India. But it is surely premature to forecast the shape of India's party system. While support for Mrs. Gandhi's Congress (I) grows, the regular Congress wrestles with the threat of defections, the relationship between the two Congress parties remains unclear, and the Janata party grapples with its own internal divisions, the party system seems likely to remain fluid.

New Directions

The diversity of interests and the variety of ideological orientations within the Janata government made it unlikely that the government would strike out in any bold new policy directions. But during its early months in office some important changes in tone and style suggested that in both domestic and foreign affairs there might be noticeable policy shifts. The government terminated arrangements for the Soviet Union to provide technical assistance for the steel plant at Bokaro and sought instead consulting assistance from American firms; the prime minister announced that the government did not intend to conduct any further nuclear explosions at this time; the minister of commerce decided to liberalize and simplify import procedures, especially for small-scale industries, and to remove restrictions on the interstate movement of wheat, thereby permitting private trade. The government also indicated that in budget allocations, more attention would be given to agriculture, irrigation, and small-scale and rural industries as part of a major effort both to strengthen the rural sector and to increase employment. The impression was widespread, too, that the Janata government intended to reduce state intervention in the economy and to take a more liberal attitude toward both domestic and foreign capital.

By the end of 1977, however, it was apparent that the Janata economic policy, while placing more emphasis on rural development and labor-intensive industries than previous governments, involved no fundamental changes in economic outlook. The Janata program continued the earlier policies of relying upon bureaucratic allocations for investment and government-controlled markets rather than on market mechanisms. The Janata party economic policy statement issued in November 1977 provided for a ceiling and floor on land holdings; greater allocations for rural development, labor intensive industries, and village and cottage industries; restrictions on capital-intensive enterprises for the manufacturing of consumer goods so as to encourage cottage industries; restrictions on investment in large urban centers in order to encourage the growth of smaller towns; the freezing of the industrial capacities of foreign firms to strengthen indigenous firms; and curbs on the growth of the twenty major industrial houses.[4]

The new government inherited from its predecessor some 18 million tons of food grain in storage and a favorable foreign exchange balance. But it also faced a spate of industrial strikes and new student

---

[4] *Statesman*, November 16, 1977.

disturbances on campuses. While government leaders attributed these to the "uncorking effect" of the regime's liberalization, it was apparent that many grievances remained to be dealt with.

On the horizon lay the threat of increased inflation, the persistent (and growing) problem of unemployment, aggravated as the number of young people entering the labor force rises each year, an unprofitable and inefficient public sector, resources inadequate to cope with these problems, and growing popular demands. As Girilal Jain, editor of the *Times of India*, wrote in June 1977:

> The political system is facing a host of serious problems. Three powerful groups—government employees, the workers in both private and public sector undertakings and the students—whom Mrs. Gandhi had put down with a heavy hand during the emergency are, for example, beginning to assert themselves. . . . The people . . . want both stable prices and a quick increase in job opportunities which is difficult to envisage without a substantial increase in development expenditure and consequently without restoring either heavy taxation, which is bound to be self-defeating even in the short run, or deficit financing on a much bigger scale than has already been the case for years. Similarly, the people want a sharp reduction in the size and power of the bureaucracy and at the same time expect it to exercise detailed control of economic activities and increase the number of white-collar jobs so that fresh graduates can be absorbed.[5]

Jain warned that the extreme politicization of the country was bound to bring the "primacy of politics over economics"—and the dual dangers of populism and repression.

The resource problem is a major constraint that will affect not only the capacity of the central government to deal with inequality, high unemployment, and low economic growth but also relations between the central government and the states. The new government soon discovered that in the months before the elections, budget deficits had been growing in almost all the states, aggravated by concessions made by the Congress governments that the new Janata governments would find politically difficult to repudiate. Perhaps as an indication of what was to follow, the finance minister announced that the compulsory deposit scheme would be continued for another two years for middle- and upper-income groups.

It seems likely that both the government and the Janata party

[5] Girilal Jain, "Coping with New Dangers—The Rising Tide of Popular Demands," *Times of India*, June 1, 1977.

will face a host of conflicting pressures springing from the resource issue. Some will seek to raise direct taxes; they will be opposed by those who fear that a tax increase would simply diminish private savings for investment. Some will demand that the center press the states to raise more funds to meet the states' budgetary needs, while others in the states will fear the political consequences of taxing agrarian interests. Those who would risk deficits in order to accelerate investment and/or income distribution programs will clash with those who want to avoid the political risks of inflation by balancing the budget. And those who wish to seek additional resources, either public or private, from abroad will meet opposition from those who favor greater reliance upon internal resources.

Beyond the resource issues there are sharp cleavages within the Janata party over the respective roles of the private and public sectors, the future of foreign investment and multinational corporations, the relative importance of large industries and of small and cottage industries, the balance between agriculture and industry, the importance of land reform as opposed to measures to stimulate the productivity of large farms, and, more generally, the relative weight to be given to equity and to growth-oriented policies. Though these differences reflect ideological preferences they also reflect the varied interests represented by the constituent elements of the Janata party. The Jana Sangh has close ties to lower-middle-class Hindus and to Hindu shopkeepers and traders throughout northern India which make them sensitive to the needs of small entrepreneurs. The Bharatiya Lok Dal, with its ties to the wealthier agricultural classes in northern India, is committed to rural development, but is less concerned with promoting equity-oriented policies than with providing security and incentives to peasant proprietors. The Socialists, though distributionists in outlook, have strong ties to the trade union movement which make them particularly responsive to the demands of organized labor. And sections of the Congress O. have close ties to the business community, though they too reaffirm their support for the public sector and for the regulation of the larger business houses.

But if the absence of a consensus on economic policy within the Janata party makes it difficult to formulate a coherent policy, it does not follow that the party or the government will necessarily disintegrate. Both the Jana Sangh and the BLD, the two most powerful elements within the party, are eager to keep Janata intact, if only because neither group could remain in power without the other so long as the Congress party stands in opposition. Jana Sanghites in particular recognize that, as the group within Janata that has the most effective local organizational base, they may well be able to increase their influence within Janata, especially when the party's present elders leave the scene.

In many respects the Janata party resembles the Congress party it displaced: it embraces divergent interests and ideologies, bound together by a concern for remaining in power; patronage therefore is important as an incentive for party loyalty and as the basis for building local party organizations; factional conflict persists within each of the state party organizations, and tensions have arisen between sections of the state and national party leadership; the party's leadership is concerned with balancing interests, ideologies, and personal ambitions even at the expense of policy coherence, and, therefore, the government's declarations of intent and its actual policies and programs sometimes widely diverge.

Thus, the elections not only restored the independence of the press, the judiciary, and the political organizations, but they also restored—in a new guise—the pattern of national and state party government that characterized India in the 1950s and early 1960s prior to the Congress party's split and its subsequent centralization under Mrs. Gandhi. In at least three respects, however, the situation is not the same as it was in the mid 60s when a decentralized Congress party governed: (1) Janata lacks a single leader who commands respect and authority throughout the party; (2) Janata's electoral and leadership base is not yet fully national in the absence of any significant strength in south India; and (3) Janata is confronted with a strong opposition, since Congress won more than a third of the vote, holds half as many parliamentary seats as Janata, and continues to be a formidable force in the state legislative assemblies.

Janata is in a somewhat more precarious position than was the Congress in the 1950s and early 60s. The death of any of its senior leaders could create a leadership vacuum over which the various constituent groups within Janata would probably clash. Janata's vulnerability to fragmentation may grow; many former Socialists and Jana Sanghites will resent the influx of former Congressmen. A recurrence of inflation, the growth of corruption, a falling out among the senior leadership could jeopardize what, for the moment at least, is India's stable center. Any one of several not improbable scenarios could plunge India into another national crisis: an open clash for national power by contending elements within the Janata party; a weak and divided center in conflict with state governments over central-state relations; a breakdown in one or more state governments leading to the imposition of central control over local opposition.

Problems will abound, as they do in any country as complex, diversified, and poor as India, but they will be tackled once again in an open political arena. Whatever the future brings it is clear that India has made a remarkable reaffirmation of its commitment to democracy. The collapse of the authoritarian government of Indira Gandhi reversed the notion that democracy alone is fragile. The election itself—a unique instance of an authoritarian regime's testing its popularity in a free election—called into question the credibility of authoritarian leaders in all Third World and Communist countries who claim that their governments rest on popular support, particularly from the poorest elements of society. The events in India challenge any authoritarian government that asserts its popular support to prove its credibility in an election as free as the one declared and lost by Indira Gandhi.

APPENDIXES

APPENDIX A

Proclamation of Emergency

This address was delivered on All India Radio on June 26, 1975, by Prime Minister Indira Gandhi.

The President has proclaimed Emergency. This is nothing to panic about.

I am sure you are all conscious of the deep and widespread conspiracy which has been brewing ever since I began to introduce certain progressive measures of benefit to the common man and woman of India. In the name of democracy it has been sought to negate the very functioning of democracy. Duly elected governments have not been allowed to function and in some cases force has been used to compel members to resign in order to dissolve lawfully elected Assemblies. Agitations have surcharged the atmosphere, leading to violent incidents. The whole country was shocked at the brutal murder of my Cabinet colleague, Shri L. N. Mishra.[1] We also deeply deplore the dastardly attack on the Chief Justice of India.

Certain persons have gone to the length of inciting our armed forces to mutiny and our police to rebel. The fact that our defense forces and the police are disciplined and deeply patriotic, and therefore, will not be taken in, does not mitigate the seriousness of the provocation.

The forces of disintegration are in full play and communal passions are being aroused, threatening our unity.

All manner of false allegations have been hurled at me. The

Reprinted in *Seminar*, no. 211 (March 1977), p. 12. The texts of this and the appendixes that follow are reprinted here as published.

[1] Mishra was killed by an unknown assassin while he was on tour in his native state of Bihar several months before the emergency was declared. In many speeches the prime minister referred to this assassination as the result of a political atmosphere created by the opposition parties.

Indian people have known me since my childhood. All my life has been in the service of our people. This is not a personal matter. It is not important whether I remain Prime Minister or not. However, the institution of the Prime Minister is important and the deliberate political attempt to denigrate it is not in the interest of democracy or of the nation.

We have watched these developments with utmost patience for long. Now we learn of a new programme challenging law and order throughout the country with a view to disrupt normal functioning. How can any government worth the name stand by and allow the country's stability to be imperilled? The actions of a few are endangering the rights of the vast majority. Any situation, which weakens the capacity of the national government to act decisively inside the country, is bound to encourage dangers from outside. It is our paramount duty to safeguard unity and stability. The nation's integrity demands firm action.

The threat to internal stability also affects production and prospects of economic improvement. In the last few months the determined action we have taken has succeeded in largely checking the price rise. We have been actively considering further measures to strengthen the economy and to relieve the hardship of various sections, particularly the poor and vulnerable, and those with fixed incomes. I shall announce them soon.

I should like to assure you that the new Emergency Proclamation will in no way affect the rights of law-abiding citizens. I am sure that internal conditions will speedily improve to enable us to dispense with this Proclamation as soon as possible.

I have been overwhelmed by the messages of goodwill from all parts of India and all sections of the people.

May I appeal for your continued co-operation and trust in the days ahead.

APPENDIX B

The Twenty-Point Economic Program

Shortly after the emergency was declared, Prime Minister Indira Gandhi announced a twenty-point economic program for the government. The program was presented in a broadcast on July 1, 1975.

(1) Continuance of steps to bring down prices of essential commodities. Streamlined production, procurement and distribution of essential commodities. Strict economy in Government expenditure.

(2) Implementation of agricultural land ceilings and speedier distribution of surplus land and compilation of land records.

(3) Stepping up of provision of house-sites for landless and weaker sections.

(4) Bonded labour, wherever it exists, will be declared illegal.

(5) Plan for liquidation of rural indebtedness. Legislation for moratorium on recovery of debt from landless labourers, small farmers and artisans.

(6) Review of laws on minimum agricultural wages.

(7) Five million more hectares to be brought under irrigation. National programme for use of underground water.

(8) An accelerated power programme. Super thermal stations under Central control.

(9) New development plan for development of handloom sector.

(10) Improvement in quality and supply of people's cloth.

Published as a leaflet by the All India Congress Committee, New Delhi.

(11) Socialisation of urban and urbanisable land. Ceiling on ownership and possession of vacant land and on plinth area of new dwelling units.

(12) Special squads for valuation of conspicuous construction and prevention of tax evasion. Summary trials and deterrent punishment for economic offenders.

(13) Special legislation for confiscation of smugglers' properties.

(14) Liberalisation of investment procedures. Action against misuse of import licences.

(15) New schemes for workers' association in industry.

(16) National permit scheme for road transport.

(17) Income relief to middle class—exemption limit raised to Rs. 8,000.

(18) Essential commodities at controlled prices to students in hostels.

(19) Books and stationery at controlled prices.

(20) New apprenticeship scheme to enlarge employment and training, especially of weaker sections.

APPENDIX C

Sanjay Gandhi's Five-Point Program

Sanjay Gandhi initially spelled out a four-point program "in which Congressmen could play a vital role" at a meeting of the Delhi Pradesh Congress Committee in March 1976. (See Overseas Hindustan Times, *March 18, 1976, p. 2.) A fifth point—the abolition of the dowry— was subsequently added. Sanjay Gandhi particularly emphasized the importance of the program for the Youth Congress workers. Variously worded, the Five-Point Program appeared on calendars, posters, and leaflets.*

(1) Each one teach one.

(2) Plant a tree.

(3) Eliminate dowry.

(4) Plan your family.

(5) Remove caste.

APPENDIX D

A Letter from Jail

Jayaprakash Narayan, the distinguished Gandhian socialist then imprisoned in Chandigarh, sent this open letter to the prime minister on July 27, 1975. It was circulated underground and abroad during the emergency.

Chandigarh, July 27, 1975

Dear Prime Minister,

I am appalled at press reports of your speeches and interviews. (The very fact that you have to say something every day to justify your action implies a guilty conscience.) Having muzzled the press and every kind of public dissent, you continue with your distortions and untruths without fear of criticism or contradiction. If you think that in this way you will be able to justify yourself in the public eye and damn the opposition to political perdition, you are sorely mistaken. If you doubt this, you may test it by revoking the emergency, restoring to the people their fundamental rights, restoring the freedom of the press, releasing all those whom you have imprisoned or detained for no other crime than performing their patriotic duty. Nine years, Madam, is not a short period of time for the people, who are gifted with a sixth sense, to have found you out. . . .

Having performed this unpleasant duty, may I conclude with a few parting words of advice? You know I am an old man. My life's work is done. And after Prabha's[1] going I have nothing and no one to live for. My brother and nephew have their family and my younger sister—the elder one died years ago—has her sons and daughters. I have given all my life, after finishing education, to the country and asked for nothing in return. So I shall be content to die a prisoner under your regime.

The full text of this letter is printed in *Seminar*, no. 211 (March 1977), pp. 13–16.
[1] Prabhavati Devi was Narayan's wife.

Would you listen to the advice of such a man? Please do not destroy the foundations that the fathers of the nation, including your noble father, had laid down. There is nothing but strife and suffering along the path that you have taken. You inherited a great tradition, noble values and a working democracy. Do not leave behind a miserable wreck of all that. It would take a long time to put all that together again. For it would be put together again, I have no doubt.

A people who fought British imperialism and humbled it cannot accept indefinitely the indignity and shame of totalitarianism. The spirit of man can never be vanquished, no matter how deeply suppressed. In establishing your personal dictatorship you have buried it deep. But it will rise from the grave. Even in Russia it is slowly coming up.

You have talked of social democracy. What a beautiful image those words call to the mind. But you have seen in eastern and central Europe how ugly the reality is. Naked dictatorship and, in the ultimate analysis, Russian overlordship. Please, please do not push India toward that terrible fate.

And may I ask to what purpose all these draconian measures? In order to be able to carry out your twenty points? But who was preventing you from carrying out the ten points? All the discontent, the protest, the *satyagraha*[2] were due precisely to the fact that you were not doing anything to implement your programme, inadequate as it was, to lighten the misery and burden under which the people and youth were groaning. This is what Chandra Shekhar, Mohan Dharia, Krishna Kant and their friends have been saying for which they have been punished.

You have talked of "drift" in the country. But was that due to opposition or to me? The drift was because of your lack of decision, direction and drive. You seem to act swiftly and dramatically only when your personal position is threatened. Once that is assured, the drift begins. Dear Indiraji, please do not identify yourself with the nation. You are not immortal, India is.

You have accused the opposition and me of every kind of villainy. But let me assure you that if you do the right things, for instance, your twenty points, tackling corruption at ministerial levels electoral reforms, etc., take the opposition into confidence, heed its advice, you will receive the willing co-operation of every one of us. For that you need not destroy democracy. The ball is in your court. It is for you to decide.

With these parting words, let me bid you farewell. May God be with you.

---

[2] Civil disobedience.

APPENDIX E

Reaffirming the Power of the People

Addressing the nation on All India Radio on January 18, 1977, Mrs. Gandhi made her surprise announcement that elections would be held.

It is some time since I last spoke to you on the Radio. However, through my continuous travels in various parts of the country and through the groups and large number of individuals whom I meet in Delhi and elsewhere, I have continued to be in close touch with you all. Your support, your affection and your trust enable me to serve India to the best of my ability.

On my journeys up and down the country, I have been glad to find that our people have shaken off the sense of defeatism and gloom. There is a new pride in being Indian. Indeed it can be said that in the year just completed, the nation has rediscovered its sense of purpose and its potential strength.

Some eighteen months ago, our beloved country was on the brink of disaster. Violence was openly preached. Workers were exhorted not to work, students not to study, and Government servants to break their oath. National paralysis was propagated in the name of revolution. The democratic way would have been to work towards the next elections, which were not far off.

Government had to act and did act. Without purposive Government a nation, specially a developing one, cannot survive. At that time I made it clear that the restrictions imposed would be temporary. They have been gradually eased. The leaders and many of the rank and file, who had been detained, have been released. For some time past press censorship has been relaxed and newspapers have been reporting the activities of people and parties. Restrictions could have

Published as a brochure by the Directorate of Advertising and Visual Publicity, Ministry of Information and Broadcasting, New Delhi, 1977.

been lifted earlier, had violence and sabotage been given up, had there been no attempt to stir up communal and other unrest.

This discipline and feeling of hope enabled us to initiate and pursue many policies to help those sections of the population who had not greatly benefited from development plans. The Constitution has been amended to remove impediments to policies which are designed to serve the people. We have also undertaken programmes to combat social evils such as dowry, which is a burden on our middle classes, and family planning, which aims at healthier and better-cared-for children. Any act of compulsion or harassment will be dealt with severely.

May I remind you that the Emergency was proclaimed because the nation was far from normal. Now that it is being nursed to health, we must ensure that there is no relapse.

Normality means the orderly conduct of business. This is possible only if people can live by certain codes and norms of behaviour. Democracy also has certain rules. Government functioning cannot be obstructed. None should imperil the welfare of any section of the people or the safety of the nation. If India is to live and prosper, there can be no preaching of hatred, no practising of violence, no encouragement of subversive activities or lowering of standards of public life.

The economic situation has vastly improved. Others are studying our anti-inflation strategy. Production has increased, thanks mainly to the new spirit of dedication which we see in our farmers, in our industrial workers, and in our scientists, technicians, managers, and administrators. The public has co-operated in spite of difficulties. We have resumed work on many development plans which had been interrupted by the economic crisis and political disturbances. The Twenty-Point and Five-Point Programmes have shown tangible results. Even though much remains to be done, they have generated an attitude of confidence, and have galvanised young and old. In spite of criticism, there is a new respect for our country abroad.

I am conscious of the difficulties which farmers, industrial workers and some other sections of our population are experiencing. We are studying each problem so as to find quick solutions. Cyclone, drought and floods have caused hardship in some areas. My sympathy to all those affected. In recent months prices of a few commodities have slightly increased. But we have already initiated corrective action which will soon show results.

We have the largest grain stocks in years. Elements which wish to stir up economic trouble will be sternly deal with. As long as there is close co-operation between Government and the people, our economic battles can and will be won.

Anyone can see that today the nation is more healthy, efficient and dynamic than it had been for a long time. The question now before us is how to restore substantively those political processes on which we were compelled to impose some curbs.

Change is the very law of life. This is a time of great fluidity in the world. Contemporary society is beset with dangers to which developing countries are especially vulnerable. Hence all change must be peaceful. This is the legacy of our freedom struggle and of Mahatma Gandhi and Jawaharlal Nehru.

Our system rests on the belief that governments derive their power from the people, and that the people give expression to their sovereign will every few years, freely and without hindrance, by choosing the government they want and by indicating their preference for policies. The government so chosen has their complete mandate to carry out such policies.

The present Lok Sabha was elected in 1971. The clearcut mandate of the people enabled the country to meet a combination of challenges —those created by the events in Bangladesh, by the international economic crisis, by the drought of 1972–73 and by the political events of 1974–75. Legally, the present Lok Sabha can continue for another 15 months.

But we also strongly believe that Parliament and Government must report back to the people and seek sanction from them to carry out programmes and policies for the nation's strength and welfare.

Because of this unshakable faith in the power of the people, I have advised the President to dissolve the present Lok Sabha and order fresh elections. This he has accepted. We expect polling to take place in March.

The rules of the Emergency are being further relaxed to permit all legitimate activity necessary for Recognised Parties to put forth their points of view before the people. I earnestly counsel political parties to eschew violence and refrain from vilification and calumny. People should neither believe in nor give currency to rumours and gossip.

Every election is an act of faith. It is an opportunity to cleanse public life of confusion. So let us go to the polls with the resolve to reaffirm the power of the people and to uphold the fair name of India as a land committed to the path of reconciliation, peace and progress.

My good wishes to you. For the people of India, may 1977 prove to be a year of added stability, strength and continuing achievement.

APPENDIX F

Revolt from Within

This statement was issued on February 2, 1977, by Jagjivan Ram, H. N. Bahuguna, Nandini Satpathy, K. R. Ganesh, D. N. Tiwari, and Raj Mangal Pande. A few days later they announced the formation of the Congress for Democracy, a new party allied to the Janata party against Congress.

We have supported Mrs. Indira Gandhi so far since 1969 because she had proclaimed a policy which promised to be the continuation of the best tradition of the Indian National Congress as adumbrated by Gandhiji. We extended to her unstinted loyalty and support so far because she had promised to eliminate narrow personal loyalties and bossism from the Congress organisation, had announced various progressive measures and had given the assurance of ending social disparities and uplifting the scheduled castes, scheduled tribes and the weaker sections by ending poverty as conveyed by her slogan of *"Garibi Hatao."*[1]

However, developments since the declaration of emergency in June 1975 have generated the most ominous trends in our country, which seem to be reversing not merely the promises and professions of the Indian National Congress since 1969, but decency and integrity in public life and also the rudimentary norms of democracy. The internal democracy of the Congress organisation at all levels has been not only abridged but has almost been abolished. Indiscipline within the Congress both in the organisational and parliamentary (legislative) wings has not been only tolerated but instigated and encouraged from above. The most dangerous procedures have been adopted to topple

Reprinted in *Seminar*, no. 211 (March 1977), pp. 37–38.
[1] "Eliminate poverty" was Indira Gandhi's slogan in the 1971 parliamentary elections.

those chief ministers who do not submit to the dictates of some individuals though they enjoy comfortable majorities in their respective legislature parties. Such ousters are achieved through intrigue, threat and allurement unknown in the history of the Congress. In this way a system of concentrating power in a coterie or even an individual has been ruthlessly taken recourse to. The tendencies towards despotic rule in the Congress organisations as also in the administration of the country are increasing alarmingly. The basic tenets of democracy and socialism to which the Congress has been committed since the thirties are being violated with impunity. The device of authorisation has been invented to complete the process of authoritarianism. Congressmen at all levels do not like these trends but have been overawed to silence and are living in a suffocating condition. A silent majority in the Congress is restive and impatiently waiting for a lead to resurrect democracy in the organisation and in the country. Millions of Congressmen, students, youths, peasants and workers, intellectuals and masses gladly underwent untold suffering and sacrifice at the call of the motherland to free her from foreign subjugation.

The motherland calls once again to guard and preserve democracy, to protect human values so that India and India alone becomes strong and prosperous. It is in this context that we have taken the fateful decision to appeal directly to Congressmen, to youth, to intelligentsia and to the people in general to come forward and prevent the impending reversal of the basic directions of Indian political life set out before us by the founding fathers of the republic. We are convinced that we would be open to the charge of gross dereliction of our duty and obligation to the people of our country if we did not take them into confidence at this decisive hour.

Any suffering for the sake of the cause will not be shirked. We have faith in the people. We have chosen this moment to appeal to them in view of the fact that the coming general elections to the Lok Sabha provide perhaps the last opportunity for preventing the total reversal of the nation's cherished policies and for correcting the illegitimacy that predominates in several aspects of our national life. We are, however, convinced that conditions are yet to be created for a free expression of the popular will and as such we demand in unequivocal terms:

—the immediate withdrawal of the emergency.
—the repeal of MISA.
—the release of all political prisoners held under arbitrary laws.
—the repeal of the Prevention of Publication of Objectionable Matters Act.

—the restoration of the Feroze Gandhi Act ensuring immunity for the publication of parliamentary proceedings.

—the declaration by the Government that the police and para-military forces shall not be used in the election in any manner that may intimidate the voters.

—the Government machinery shall not be used in any manner for the purpose of promoting the interest and image of any person in political life.

—the Government's mass media, particularly the radio and the television, shall observe the norms that prevailed before the emergency.

Any party believing in parliamentary system of Government cannot possibly consider going to the electorate to seek legitimacy for itself without fulfilling these minimum conditions for a free expression of the popular verdict.

We appeal to all right-thinking Congressmen, who cherish the democratic traditions of the Congress organisation to seriously consider the grave impairment of democratic norms and procedures which has recently afflicted the Congress organisation. Many duly elected Congress committees at *pradesh* and district levels have been arbitrarily replaced by ad hoc committees. The AICC,[2] which has always been a predominantly elected body having only 10 percent nominated members with no voting rights, has of late, been reduced to a submissive ratifying committee with nearly half of its members selected by nomination. Political and organisational decisions of grave consequences have been announced at random by persons having no locus standi in the Congress organisation and such decisions have often been taken behind the back of even the Congress Working Committee. Therefore, now is the time for all Congressmen to assert themselves openly, and with the aid of the people, who hold the Indian National Congress as the repository of their emergence to nationhood, to reverse the current drift to disaster.

We appeal to all right-thinking Congressmen, who have the interests of India's toiling millions in their heart, to realise that the 20-point programme has virtually been pushed to the background, thanks to the emphasis on certain new programmatic points and through a whole series of major concessions granted to vested interests, while denying the working class their rightful claims. In this connection, it is necessary to visualise the grave consequences of the manner in which land reforms have been relegated to a secondary

---

[2] The All India Congress Committee, the national governing council of the Congress party.

position and the way the rule of law for all practical purposes has yielded place to rule of men. This has seriously eroded the credibility of the highest authorities of the land on the one hand and has created grave feeling of insecurity in the minds of the poor masses as well as the minority communities on the other. The very purpose of all our social and economic programme is being defeated and the common people are being alienated from the Congress and the Government.

We are convinced that a leadership which alienates the minorities and the have-nots from the Congress organisation is throwing to the winds the most important plans of the Indian National Congress and the Indian political system. We have chosen to come out openly at this hour also because we feel that such grave impairment of the confidence of the minorities may ultimately disrupt the integrity of the nation itself. We shall do all in our power to restore the confidence of the minorities and the weaker section of the people.

We would like to reiterate that our objective is the defence of the best tradition of the Indian National Congress. The restoration of decency and integrity in public life, the prevention of the current drift of our democratic system in the direction of a regime of authoritarian and self-centered establishment. We have decided to stand by the long suffering people of this country, the poor and the deprived, no matter what price we have to pay.

In this solemn endeavour we seek the active co-operation of all forward looking forces of our country and we appeal to all right-thinking Congressmen to respond to the call of their conscience. This is a crucial moment when the defence of democracy is the supreme task facing our nation. We go into this crusade with unflinching faith in our people and in the triumph of our cause.

APPENDIX G

The Congress Party Manifesto

Through every crucial stage of the history of India in the twentieth century and in each momentous crisis which the nation has faced, the Indian National Congress has provided great and inspiring leadership through such illustrious figures as Mahatma Gandhi, Jawaharlal Nehru, Vallabhbhai Patel, Abul Kalam Azad, Rajendra Prasad and Subhas Chandra Bose. It has provided bold initiatives and unflinching dedication and service to the people at all times. The Indian National Congress has always been a party of the masses, a party of the people, a party in the vanguard of progress, wedded to the cause of the poor.

2. The Indian National Congress was the first to question the right of an alien authority to rule over India, first to voice the people's yearning for liberty, first to launch the struggle for freedom, first to oppose communalism and espouse the ideal of secularism, first to pledge the nation to democracy, first to resolve to end poverty, first to fight for economic and social justice, first to adopt socialism as a national goal and first to lead the country from backwardness into the modern age.

3. Through three decades of freedom, the Indian National Congress has stood steadfast by the ideals that inspired the liberation struggle and to the principles that have activated the Indian Revolution. It has resolutely rebuffed every attempt made, internally and externally, to undermine and undo the great purposes of the nation. It has squarely faced the latest desperate attack made upon the people. Despite the continuing threat, Congress, with undiminished faith in the people, calls upon all citizens to give it a clear and unequivocal

Published by the All India Congress Committee, New Delhi, 1977.

mandate to carry the nation forward unitedly to peace, progress and prosperity through democracy, secularism and socialism, safeguarding the integrity of the nation.

4. The record of the Indian National Congress in the years of freedom has been steadily to enlarge the power of the people. Democratic institutions have been built and nurtured. In the policy and decision making processes the voice of the people has been made supreme. Spectacular progress has been made in agriculture and industry, in science, education and public health. In many areas our scientific and technological competence is comparable to that of the foremost industrialised countries. Today we have the third largest technical manpower in the world. Backward regions have been opened up and new opportunities brought to disabled sections, especially Harijans, tribals and backward classes oppressed by centuries of discrimination. We are now in a position to launch a successful attack on age-long poverty. India is one of the few countries in the world which has set up specific and daring social and economic targets in the face of unimaginable odds. Recent months have shown that the political capacity and economic strength so built by the Indian National Congress can be put to the greatest advantage of the people through self-confident, self-reliant, disciplined and dedicated functioning.

5. In the 1971 elections, the people reiterated their faith in the Congress ideals of democracy, secularism and socialism. The Congress manifesto had promised to continue the advance to socialism, to subdue the forces of violence and disorder, to safeguard the interests of the minorities and weaker sections, to end privy purses and other such privileges, to provide new employment avenues, to enlarge the role and efficiency of the public sector to give proper scope to the private sector to play a national role without concentration of economic power to control prices and ensure supplies of essential commodities, to launch a vigorous programme of child welfare, to expand and improve education and, for these purposes, to amend the Constitution suitably.

6. Congress has redeemed these promises in substantial measure, thanks to its firm, resolute and farsighted leadership and the will of the people. This has been done in the face of the heavy burden, dislocation and distraction caused by the crisis in Bangladesh and the ensuing war forced upon the country in 1971, the international economic crisis since 1971, the severe droughts of 1972 and 1973, and the attempts by the opposition parties to obstruct and subvert Government and our democratic institutions.

7. Most of the parties which have now entered into alliances or adjustments against the Congress had in 1971 combined under the name of the Grand Alliance. These parties wedded to communalism, reaction or left extremism had different and even conflicting ideologies and programmes. They united only to oppose the progressive policies of the Congress. Spurned by the people in the Parliamentary elections of 1971 and the State elections of 1972, and alarmed and enraged by the various progressive measures of the Government, certain opposition parties took to extraconstitutional agitation. In 1973 and 1974 these parties, exploiting economic difficulties and the impact of global inflation stirred up discontent to bring about the dissolution of elected legislative assemblies. In the name of democracy, but in collusion with anti-social elements, they sought to negate the working of democracy. By resorting to force, duress and brutal violence, duly elected governments were not allowed to function.

8. In this surcharged atmosphere, certain opposition leaders went to the length of inciting the armed forces to mutiny and the police and government officials to rebel. Forces of disintegration were unleashed and communal passions were roused threatening the very unity and integrity of the country. No government could have stood by and allowed the country's stability and integrity to be so imperilled.

9. Freedom does not include the licence to undermine national interests. But the aim of these opposition parties was to paralyse national activity and the Government itself and to usurp power by unconstitutional means. The Constitution-makers, envisaging precisely such internal disorders, had provided for the declaration of an emergency under the Constitution. No option was left but to declare an emergency when such a situation did arise. This timely and necessary measure was ratified by Parliament. It saved the Republic from catastrophe and restored political stability.

[Points 10 through 40 describe the accomplishments of the Congress government in domestic and international affairs.]

41. The Congress appeals to the people to return its candidates to the Lok Sabha in the 1977 elections with a massive majority, so that it can:

1. uphold the ideals of secularism, protect the interests of the minorities and the right of every community to pursue its faith and way of life,

2. preserve and consolidate democracy and put an end to all forms of violence and disorder, so that people can live in peace and harmony,

3. fight poverty, ignorance, disease and inequality and build a modern, prosperous, egalitarian and socialist society,

4. abolish all kinds of discrimination between one human being and another and end all forms of exploitation,

5. develop and modernise agriculture and allied activities, expediate integrated rural development programmes and bring about a total rural regeneration,

6. promote the interests of the small and marginal farmers, agricultural workers, Scheduled Castes and Scheduled Tribes, and backward classes and communities,

7. strengthen and diversify the country's industrial base, enlarge the role of the public sector, give scope to the private sector to play its due role within the priorities of the Plan and without bringing about a concentration of economic wealth and power,

8. take up a massive programme to expand opportunities for productive employment,

9. protect the interests of the working class and give them their proper share in management and the fruits of their labour,

10. keep prices in check and ensure essential commodities to the people at reasonable prices,

11. provide primary education to all children and improve the scope of secondary and higher education,

12. expand health and medical facilities and welfare programmes for the people.

42. The motto of the Congress is: poverty must go, disparity must diminish and injustice must end. The Congress renews its pledge to the people to work and toil, ceaselessly and without respite, to build a society worthy of our great nation and reflecting the vision of Mahatma Gandhi and Jawaharlal Nehru.

43. The purpose of the elections must be to provide the nation with a government at the Centre strong enough to safeguard India's independence and interests in a rapidly changing world, wise enough to preserve the legacy of tolerance and peaceful change, and determined enough to carry forward the recent gains so that, with the self-reliant technological strength already gained, the nation can march forward.

44. In the words of the Prime Minister, "Every election is an act of faith. It is an opportunity to cleanse public life of confusion. So, let us go to the polls with the resolve to reaffirm the power of the people and to uphold the fair name of India as a land committed to the path of reconciliation, peace and progress."

45. The Indian National Congress alone has the dynamism, the policy, the programme, the leadership and the achievement displayed through ninety-one years of sustained and devoted service to the people of India.

Congress is the people! Vote for Congress.

APPENDIX H

The Janata Party Manifesto

Both Bread and Liberty: A Gandhian Alternative

The forthcoming Lok Sabha poll constitutes the most crucial election that the country has had since Independence. The choice before the electorate is clear. It is a choice between freedom and slavery; between democracy and dictatorship; between abdicating the power of the people or asserting it; between the Gandhian path and the way that has led many nations down the precipice of dictatorship, instability, military adventure and national ruin.

Our people are being asked to make this choice in most abnormal circumstances. The Emergency that was declared on June 25, 1975 has not been withdrawn. The sweeping and draconian powers with which the Government armed itself, remain intact. Fundamental rights have not been restored. The citizen has no protection against arbitrary arrest and indefinite incarceration. The courts have been deprived of vital powers. MISA, with all its obnoxious provisions, continues in force. The Prevention of Publication of Objectionable Matters Act has been entrenched in the Constitution. The Press is not free. Thousands of political workers are still under detention in different parts of the country. The Constitution has been amended and laws fashioned to sanctify the ruling party's definition of a "committed" judiciary, a "committed" press and a "committed" bureaucracy. The monopolistic control of All India Radio, Doordarshan[1] and Samachar, that involuntarily "nationalised" news agency, is being used to convert these mass media into instruments of party propaganda and to

Published by the Janata party, New Delhi, 1977. These excerpts are taken from pp. 1–3, 9–11, 17–18, 24–25, and 26.

[1] Government-run television.

deny the Opposition fair opportunity to present its point of view to the people.

The Government has made this crucial election a grossly unequal contest in relation to time, resources and the continuing application of emergency provisions. History is replete with instances where those who conspire against the rights of the people attempt to undermine freedom by portraying it as a luxury, dear only to those who wish to defend property and privilege. They cleverly conceal the fact that fundamental freedoms are weapons that the oppressed and the poor need to fight tyranny, exploitation and injustice, vested interests and opportunist governments. Bread cannot be juxtaposed against liberty. The two are inseparable.

Nightmare of Fear

The months through which the country has passed since the declaration of the so-called internal emergency have been a nightmare of fear and humiliation, reminiscent of the days of foreign domination. A fresh emergency was invoked after the judgement of the Allahabad High Court and the verdict of the people in Gujarat. Behind the cover of censorship, a reign of terror was unleashed with the massive deployment of police and para-military forces. Indiscriminate arrests became the order of the day. A pall of fear was thrown over the country. The rule of law ceased to exist. The right of habeas corpus was taken away. The judicial process was gravely undermined and the citizen was placed at the mercy of the State. The courts were solemnly told that while the emergency lasted, they were powerless to protect the citizen even if he should be starved to death or shot. The concept of equality before law, precious to any democratic society, was jettisoned, and a constitutional amendment was sought to be enacted to confer immunity on the individual holding the office of Prime Minister. The Representation of the People Act was amended to redefine corrupt practices and to legalise what was considered and found corrupt before the emergency. The Press was gagged. Hundreds of printing presses were sealed. Papers and journals were compelled to close down. The academic world was not left untouched. Innumerable teachers and students were arrested. All democratic rights were whittled away.

Extra-Constitutional Power Centres

Extra-constitutional centres of power were built up in the Government and permitted to wield enormous official power without the trammels of legality or accountability. Consummate efforts were made to destroy the distinction between party and State that characterises a democratic polity.

Onslaught on Working Class

The worker found his cherished and hard-won rights eroded. Even the tardy increase in his dearness allowance was impounded. He was robbed of his bonus. The instruments of power were abused to suppress or subvert independent trade unions. Trade union workers were thrown into jail and attempts were made to manipulate union elections and bring these organisations under the control of the ruling party. While workers were denied the right to strike, employers were left free to declare lock-outs and to lay off workers with impunity, and aided to fatten on new concessions and new agreements with multinationals.

42nd Amendment

The Constitution was amended to sanctify and institutionalise a total concentration of power in the hands of one individual—the Prime Minister. The authoritarian trends that had unfolded themselves over the past few years were embodied in the 42nd Amendment which was bulldozed through Parliament. To call it an amendment is a misnomer. It is a betrayal of the testament of faith that the founding fathers bequeathed to the people and it subverts the basic structure of the 1950 Constitution. It vitiates the federal principle and upsets the nice balance between the people and Parliament, Parliament and the judiciary, the judiciary and the executive, the States and the Centre, the citizen and the Government. It is the culmination of a conspiracy to devalue democracy that started with the erosion of the cabinet system, the deliberate and consummate scuttling of democratic processes in the ruling party, and the concentration of all power in the hands of a leader who has been sought to be identified with the nation or even to be placed above it.

The Emergency has succeeded only in generating an atmosphere of fear and insecurity. The question before the electorate is whether whatever might have been achieved during the past 19 months was achieved because of the emergency or whether the price of freedom, human rights and long-term economic and social destabilisation that the country has had to pay was necessary for, or commensurate with, whatever has supposedly been achieved. . . .

Political Charter

As a party wedded to the ideals of freedom and democracy, it believes that fearlessness is of the essence. It will therefore take immediate steps to free the people from the bondage of fear. It will restore to the citizen his fundamental freedoms and to the judiciary its rightful role.

To generate fearlessness and to revive democracy, the Janata Party will:

(1) Lift the emergency;

(2) Restore the fundamental freedoms that have been suspended by Presidential Order;

(3) Repeal MISA, release all political detenues, and review all other unjust laws;

(4) Enact laws to ensure that no political or social organisation is banned without independent judicial enquiry;

(5) Seek to rescind the 42nd Amendment;

(6) Amend Article 352 of the Constitution to prevent its abuse in the interest of an individual or group;

(7) Move to amend Article 356 to ensure that the power to impose President's Rule in the States is not misused to benefit the ruling party or any favoured faction within it;

(8) Introduce electoral reforms after a careful consideration of suggestions made by various committees including the Tarkunde Committee and, in particular, consider proposals for recall of errant legislators and for reducing election costs, as well as for reducing the voting age from 21 to 18;

(9) Repeal the amendment to the Representation of the People Act which redefines corrupt practices and places electoral offences by certain individuals beyond the scrutiny of the courts;

(10) Re-establish the rule of law;

(11) Restore the authority of the judiciary and safeguard the independence and integrity of the Bar;

(12) Ensure that all individuals, including those who hold high office, are equal before law;

(13) Assure the right to peaceful and non-violent protest;

(14) Abolish censorship and end all harassment to newspapers, journals, publishers and printing presses;

(15) Safeguard the freedom of the press by repealing the Prevention of Publication of Objectionable Matters Act, and restore the immunity that the Press previously enjoyed in reporting legislative proceedings;

(16) Ensure that All-India Radio, Doordarshan and the Films Division are converted into genuinely autonomous bodies that are politically objective and free from governmental interference;

(17) Ensure that news agencies are completely independent of the Government and are not given the right to monopoly;

(18) Delete property from the list of Fundamental Rights and, instead, affirm the right to work;

(19) Ensure that Government employees are not victimised, are freed of political pressure, and are not compelled to execute illegal orders and unlawful actions. Their right to access to Courts will be restored.

A New Economic Policy

Social justice is not an abstract concept indicating good intentions, but is a basic philosophy which must be translated into action and lead to the welfare of the masses on the principle of equality and prosperity for all. There cannot be two societies, rich and poor, in which the latter category is made to subserve the goals of elitism, consumerism and urbanism. The Gandhian values of *"antyodaya"*[2] and austerity must be accepted and implemented if the vicious circle of the poor becoming poorer and the rich richer is to be broken. Hence the Janata Party affirms the right to work. This can become a realisable ideal only if we move towards the establishment of an economy in which agriculture and cottage and small industries have primacy, and are not sacrificed to the big machine and the big city. Modernisation of industry must be based on improved technology. But the only way to steer clear of the evils of capitalism and state capitalism and to ensure full employment and the decentralisation of economic power is to follow the Gandhian precept that whatever can be produced efficiently by decentralised industry should be so produced. There is room for heavy and large-scale industry, but only where it is not possible to organise such production satisfactorily in

---

[2] Literally, "the rise of the last man"—that is, the well-being of the poorest.

138

the cottage and small scale sector. This spirit must inform the nation's economic policy. . . .

Economic Charter

The Janata Party's Economic Programme envisages:

(1) Deletion of property as a fundamental right;

(2) Affirmation of the right to work and a full employment strategy;

(3) Stress on Gandihan values of austerity, *"antyodaya"* and a decentralised economy;

(4) An end to destitution within ten years;

(5) Appropriate technology for self-reliance;

(6) New planning priorities, notably the primacy of agriculture, agrarian reforms and more favourable terms of trade and higher allocations for the rural sector;

(7) Narrowing down of rural-urban disparities and a new rural-urban nexus;

(8) Emphasis on wage goods production for mass consumption;

(9) Statutory reservation of spheres of production for small-scale and cottage industries;

(10) A wage and price policy; raising the minimum tax exemption limit to Rs. 10,000 and exemption of land revenue on all holdings below 2.5 hectares;

(11) Redistributive taxation and excise in lieu of sales tax;

(12) Formulation of a national water policy and a national energy policy;

(13) Environmental care. . . .

Social Charter

The Janata Party's Social Charter will comprise:

(1) Education reform with middle schooling for all within 12 years;

(2) Eradication of illiteracy;

(3) Safe drinking water for all;

(4) Stress on community and preventive health, and measures towards group health insurance;

(5) A New Village movement;

(6) Low-cost building and mass public housing;

(7) A policy regarding urbanisation;

(8) A comprehensive scheme of social insurance;

(9) Family planning as part of a larger population policy package, without coercion;

(10) A new deal for the scheduled castes and tribes with special machinery to guarantee their rights and interests;

(11) A Civil Rights Commission;

(12) Automatic machinery for combating corruption;

(13) Women's rights and youth welfare;

(14) Legal aid and inexpensive justice;

(15) Fostering people's initiative and voluntary action. . . .

Faith in the Future

The Janata Party has faith in the future of India because it has unstinted faith in the Indian people—their traditions, their values, their courage, their humanism and their dedication. The people know just how near the precipice the country has been brought by our present rulers, and for what ends.

Steeled by this experience and determined to live as free people, the Janata Party calls on every citizen to rally and fight the tyranny so that we may all, with goodwill and civility, join together in building the future: a free and just society.

ONWARD TO VICTORY, FREEDOM, PROGRESS

APPENDIX I

A Call for Total Revolution

In this broadcast on April 14, 1977, Jayaprakash Narayan called for "total revolution" against social evils.

My dear countrymen, many friends have been pressing me in the past few months to say something to the nation. Being bed-ridden and, therefore, out of touch with the objective situation in the country, I have been hesitating to say anything.

Only a few days ago, the Prime Minister spoke to the nation. After her excellent discourse, I should have thought there was no need for any other voice to be raised. But friends still think that the Prime Minister having spoken as the Head of Government, there was need for a common citizen like me to speak on behalf of the people.

While I disclaim any authority to speak for the people, I am placing here my views as a common citizen.

The first observation that I should like to make and emphasise is, that the results of the last general election were due to the students' and people's movement that had started from Gujarat and spread to Bihar and whose message had resounded throughout the country.

The essence of that message was that an elected representative of the people does not necessarily require a right to hold on to his position until the expiry of his legal term.

The principle that was asserted during the movement was that when an individual representative or a representative government failed in duty, became corrupt and oppressive and inefficient, the electors, i.e. the people, had a right to demand their resignation irrespective of the time they may yet have left to serve.

Printed in *Times of India*, April 14, 1977.

The example of ex-President Richard Nixon of the United States, illustrates the proposition I am enunciating here.

It is true that what is called the "right of recall" has no place in our Constitution. But in a democracy, the people have an unwritten right, which they can exercise if and when necessary.

All this does not mean that any small number of disgruntled persons have the right to demand an elected representative or government to step down from office whenever they wish.

But it does mean that if it is found beyond any doubt that a vast majority of the people concerned are convinced of the corruption, nepotism and inefficiency of a government or an elected representative and demand their resignation, the people's voice must prevail.

It is possible that the party in power, or the individual representative concerned, might also mobilise their supporters, but if there is a genuine people's upsurge against them, democratic ethics and practice require that the will of the people, the great majority, must prevail over that of a small minority.

To the constitutionalists this may appear to be an anarchic proposition. However, it should be remembered that practically every major constitution in the world was drafted in the wake of revolutionary upheavals.

This is a good occasion to look back and recall how the student's movement against corruption in Gujarat had assumed an all-India character. Political and governmental corruption was the central point of the people's movement. Therefore, it is the duty of those who have come to power in the wake of that movement to take some concrete and effective steps to stop and root out corruption from these spheres.

It is my view that just like the High Courts and the Supreme Court, there should be an autonomous institution set up with legal authority and rights both at the Centre and in the states. The Swedish Ombudsman naturally comes to one's mind, but in the Indian conditions some broader kind of institution seems to be necessary.

For instance, at the Centre a body that may be known as Lokpal might be set up consisting of not more than five members with powers to hold investigations on their own initiative as well as on the initiative of any citizen or any private or public body.

A group of individual jurists might be entrusted with the task of drawing up a blueprint of such a body and a clause to this effect might be inserted in the Constitution. These are my first expectations from the government.

The main issue raised by the students-cum-people's movement was electoral and administrative reforms so as to make elections cheap and truly representative and bring the administration nearer to the people.

Another important demand concerns educational reforms so as to relate education to the problems of the country and fit the educated to deal with them. It was also desired that a medium of education should be made universal and illiteracy and ignorance banished from the land.

The charter of demands that I placed before the Speaker of the Lok Sabha and the President (Chairman) of the Rajya Sabha on behalf of the people on March 6, 1975, deserves to be reproduced here so that it may serve as a standard by which to measure the work and functioning of the present government.

Except for the Centre, the Congress governments still continue to function in the states. It is necessary as soon as possible to give a chance to the people to elect their fresh representatives who would be committed to the people's charter in addition to their election manifestoes.

It will be recalled that the ultimate objective of the people's movement was defined by me as total revolution. This term "total revolution" was derided by some at that time and brushed aside by some others as a dream of an impractical person.

Therefore, I should like to repeat my faith in what I called total revolution and pledge myself to work for it as soon as my health permits.

In our heritage from the past there are some things that are noble and valuable. They have to be preserved and strengthened. But we have also inherited a great deal of superstition and wrong values and unjust human and social relations.

The caste system among the Hindus is a glaring example of our evil inheritance. From the time of Lord Buddha, and maybe from even earlier times, attempts have been made to destroy the hierarchical system of caste but it still flourishes in every part of the country. It is time that we blotted out this black spot from the Hindu society and proclaimed and practised the equality and brotherhood of all men.

Similarly, there are rotten customs and manners associated with such things as marriage, birth, death, etc. The purging of these evils also falls within the purview of the total revolution.

Coming to more modern spheres of life, such as education, it is time that the radical recommendations of the several education commissions, the Kothari Commission not being the least of them, are implemented.

Here we might follow the example of China, in which all the schools and colleges were closed down and the students were sent out to the villages and slums of the towns to impart the rudiments of education to every citizen, young or old.

I have not said anything here about the usual socio-economic reforms that are so much talked about but about which so little has actually been done. For this task, too, youth power can be drafted with advantage to the youth themselves and to society at large.

Finally, if God grants me better health in the coming months, I look forward to take up my cry of total revolution and do whatever might lie in my power.

In the meanwhile, the work need not be stopped. Let everyone do his bit, singly or in cooperation with others.

Here is a beacon light for our youth. I hope they will steer the course of their life towards that light.

I am at their disposal even in my sick bed for advice and such guidance as I might be capable of giving. So, forward, my young friends. *"Sampoorn kranti ab naara hai, bhawi itihas hamara hai."*[1]

---

[1] "Total revolution is our slogan, the future is ours."

INDEX

145

146

Narain, Raj: 14, 58, 100
Narayan, Jayaprakash: 4n, 14, 16, 32, 43, 47, 60, 61, 63, 100, 101, 103, 120, 141
Nasbandi. See Sterilization campaign
National Conference, election outcome (1977), role in: 54–55, 90, 95, 102
Naxalites: 28, 80
Nehru, Jawaharlal: 2, 32
Nehru, Motilal: 2, 32
New Delhi: 6, 21, 30, 36, 58
Newspapers. *See* Press
North:
    election outcome (1977), factor in, 6, 13, 29, 35, 37, 38, 41, 42, 46–47, 48, 49, 50, 67, 69–74, 81, 87, 88, 94, 109
    Janata government, role in, 101, 106

Orissa:
    CPI in, 92
    election results, parliamentary (1971), 73; (1977), 69, 73
    election results, state assembly (1977), 101, 102, 103
    scheduled caste constituencies in, 83
    tribal constituencies in, 84
    voter turnout in (1977), 86, 87

Pakistan: 11, 53n
Palkiwala, A.: 60
Pande, Raj Mangal: 15n, 125
Pandit, Vijayalakshmi: 32
Parliamentary elections. *See* Elections
Party system:
    election outcome (1977), effect on, 55, 62, 67, 89–97, 103–106, 110–111
    emergency, effects on, 1–7, 8–12, 15–17, 28, 30–33, 40–41, 42, 44, 45, 47, 60, 87
    See also Democracy; *under individual parties*
Patel, H.M.: 100
Patel, Rajni: 30
Patel, Sardar Vallabhbhai: 2, 32
Patil, S.K.: 30
Police, political role of: 1, 3, 6, 10, 16, 36n, 57, 62, 80
Political meetings and rallies: 5, 16, 21–23, 31–32, 40–41, 42, 50
Pondicherry, election results, state assembly: 101, 102
Posters: 23–24
Praja Socialist party (PSP): 14n, 103

Prasad, Rajendra: 2
President, election of (1977): 103
President's rule: 4, 49, 51, 54
Press:
    election outcome (1977), role in, 1, 12, 21, 22–23, 37–38, 46, 49, 58, 80, 96, 110
    emergency, effects on, 4, 5–6, 8, 11, 12, 22–23, 52, 62, 96, 99
    Janata government policy toward, 62–63
Prevention of Publication of Objectionable Matters Act: 5, 63
Punjab:
    CPI in, 94
    CPM in, 94
    election outcome (1977), role in, 10, 38, 48, 86, 90–91, 94, 106
    election results, parliamentary (1971), 74; (1977), 74, 75, 77, 84
    election results, state assembly (1967), 54; (1972), 54; (1977), 102
    scheduled caste constituencies in, 83, 87, 88
    voter turnout in (1977), 86, 87, 88

Rae Bareli constituency: 58, 100
Rajasthan:
    election results, parliamentary (1971), 74; (1977), 74, 84, 87
    election results, state assembly (1977), 101, 102, 103
    scheduled caste constituencies in, 83, 87, 88
    voter turnout in (1977), 86, 87, 88
Rajya Sabha: 28, 103
Ram, Jagjivan: 14–16, 47, 60, 61, 62, 84, 100, 125
Ramachandran, M.G.: 49–50
Rashtriya Swayamsevak Sangh (RSS): 28, 40–41, 66
Ray, Siddharta Shankar: 54, 104
Reddi, Neelam Sanjiva: 103
Reddy, Brahmananda: 45, 104
Reddy, Sanjiva: 13
Regional parties: 49–55, 91–92, 96, 101–102, 103
Regional voting patterns (1977): 69–74; *see also* Voting patterns
Research and Analysis Wing (RAW): 6, 99
Reserved constituencies: 67, 69, 82–85, 87

Samachar: 4, 11, 99
Samyukta Socialist party (SSP): 14n